303 tips for detailing model railroad scenery and structures

BY DAVE FRARY AND BOB HAYDEN
PHOTOS BY DAVE FRARY

Introduction 3

Scenery tips 6

Tips for texture and trees 16

Forced perspective and backdrops 27

On the waterfront 32

Tricks with figures and vehicles 39

Detailing and superdetailing 47

Signs of life 56

Improving and detailing structures 63

Weathering and airbrushing 78

Workshop tips 87

Where to find the products 93

Bibliography 94

Index 95

KALMBACH BOOKS

Acknowledgements
Our thanks to the following fellow modelers who
graciously provided ideas, inspiration, subjects for
photos, or just plain help: Pete Laier, Dick Patterson,
Hal Reynolds, George Sellios, and Tom Wilson.

Cover design: Lisa Bergman
Cover photo: Dave Frary
Layout: Bob Hayden

Publisher's Cataloging in Publication
(Prepared by Quality Books Inc.)

Frary, Dave.
   303 tips for detailing model railroad scenery and
structures / by Dave Frary and Bob Hayden ; photos
by Dave Frary.
    p. cm. — (Model railroad handbook)
   Includes index.
   ISBN 0-89024-243-7

   1. Railroads—Models. I. Hayden, Bob. II. Title.
III. Title : Three hundred three tips for detailing
model railroad scenery and structures. IV. Title:
Three hundred three tips for detailing model railroad
scenery and structures. V. Series.

TF197.F73 1995   625.1'9
                                  QBI94-21260

Introduction

THIS IS A BOOK OF TIPS and techniques for making your model railroad more detailed and realistic. That's a fairly broad topic, and the hints included here range from ways to make better trees to ideas on what adhesives and solvents you should keep around your workbench. We've always maintained that there are no secrets to building a pleasing layout, but if there are, here are ours!

Most of the examples in the photos, like the shot of Bob Hayden's Carrabasset & Dead River Ry. shown here, are HO scale, and many of them show models on the HOn2½ layouts we've worked on over the past 30 years. Nothing here is specific to narrow gauge modeling, however, and virtually every tip can be put to work in any scale or gauge.

One theme of this book is making your railroad

different — that is, unique and interesting — by combining common commercial items with your imagination. You don't have to be a scratchbuilder. In fact, for us scratchbuilding is only a last resort, reserved only for those elements so characteristic of your prototype railroad or locale that you can't buy them or modify something you can buy.

BUILDING SCENES THAT TELL A STORY

Detail on your layout is a means to focus attention, and you should keep that principle in mind as you build. Think of your layout and the scenes within it as telling a story, then decide how detailing and finishing will support that story. Figures, like the folks shown below waiting for the train, provide an obvious way to direct attention, as do vehicles and signs, and you'll find all three discussed in the chapters that follow.

Detailing should be theatrical, and that means

it's more than just incorporating every bolt, rivet, and the precise color scheme that appears on your prototype. Effective detailing substitutes suggestions of color and texture for bolt-for-bolt modeling, admitting that appearance is more important than reality.

One aspect of effective detailing is providing visual evidence of time. Weathering is a big part of this, and the first thing most of us get into, but representing the passage of time includes more. Evidence that something's been on your layout for years augments the layout's ability to tell its story, and that time factor makes the whole scene less toylike. (Toys, after all, are bright and shiny : Everybody wants new, shiny toys, not old, weathered ones.)

We've been trying various weathering techniques for years, and still make it a point to weather everything that goes on the layout. Over the years,

though, we've started to paint down the trains a bit less than the scenery and structures. This needs to be kept subtle, but if the trains are just a bit more vibrant than their surroundings, they'll naturally "pop" out of the scene. This effect carries through in person as well as in photos.

DETAILING BY THE ZONES

Detailing is a way to achieve dramatic direction and pacing on your layout, and that means detail should be uneven. Bare spots are important, too, because they tell your viewers to focus their attention elsewhere, and emphasize the richness of detail by contrast. Even if you had the luxury of enough parts or enough time to detail every square inch of every scene, you wouldn't want to, because such detail would become a crust or frosting instead of enhancement.

No one can build a layout that's a complete miniature world, so we have to substitute dramatic composition and pacing for perfection — and that's more fun anyway! It's important for you to think of both individual scenes and your layout as a whole in terms of three zones, each of them defined by its distance from your viewer.

The foreground is the detail zone. This is where you pull out all the stops: the best detail parts, the most careful painting, and the strictest fidelity to prototype. It extends from the front edge of your layout to close-up focusing distance, maybe 16". Top-notch detail in the foreground implies the same level of refinement all the way to the back of the layout. Your lighting should be the best in this zone, too, since you don't want all your effort to go unappreciated.

From 16" in to arm's length — about 26" — is the middleground. Here, shapes and colors become more important than precise details, and you can begin to get away with suggesting detail instead of rivet-for-rivet modeling. If you've got some rough detail parts or vehicles that aren't the best, this is the place for them.

Beyond arm's length, in the background of your layout, almost anything goes. This is where outright tricks come into play: low-relief flats instead of 3-D structures, less-than-full-scale models to achieve forced perspective, and details painted on instead of modeled. You have to work from the assumption that anything back there can't truly be appreciated anyway, so it's a waste of effort to pour a lot of time into it.

The big exception to this theatrical approach is the trains. Rolling stock always has to be treated as foreground models, since every locomotive and car will eventually find its way into the critical foreground zone.

LET'S GET STARTED — AND KEEP IT LIGHT!

Building the kind of detailed model railroad scenes discussed in this book can become serious work, but it shouldn't. This hobby, and all modelbuilding, is something we do because we don't have to, and the activity is only worthwhile as long as it's fun and relaxing.

So keep it that way! You don't have to turn your railroad into a fun house (though you can if you want!), but be on the lookout for ways to make your layout reflect your sense of humor. A few light touches here and there will make the serious business of railroading seem that much more realistic.

P.S.: Although this book has two authors, we've used "I" throughout the tips that follow. It makes them easier to read — and to tell the truth, we don't always know who invented which one, anyway.

Elephants on the Carrabasset & Dead River? You bet — hey, maybe the circus is coming to town! No matter how detailed your layout becomes, be sure to reserve at least a little room for a belly laugh or two!

Dave built *Model Railroader*'s Pennsylvania Railroad project layout, which was featured in the magazine during 1993.

1

Scenery tips

Making your scenery special — from terrain to retaining walls

THE NUMBER-ONE TREND of the past 20 years in model railroading is scenery. More layouts than ever before have scenery, and it's good-looking scenery, too. I think this is because new techniques and easy-to-use products have come along to make the job easier, but I also think that more and more model railroaders have come to realize how important scenery is in making a layout enjoyable.

Effective scenery doesn't have to be built to scale in the same sense that cars and locomotives are. In fact, it can't be. Scenery just has to look good. Here are tips to make yours look better than ever.

SCENIC BASE MATERIALS

Over the years, just about everything imaginable has been used to make the basic scenic contour shell. Here's a rundown of the popular methods that I'd call still workable.

Screen wire. Way back when, common steel window screening was draped over wood blocks for support, then pushed into shape for the terrain. The wire was held in place with carpet tacks or staples. The two disadvantages I found were that the sharp ends of the wire made my hands look like pincushions, and the wire rusted, leaving brown streaks on the scenery. Many modelers still use screen wire today, but they substitute modern aluminum or fiberglass screening.

Cardboard strips. Another old favorite, and the scenic base material I've used the most (and still use) is cardboard strips. Cut 1"-wide strips from corrugated boxes with a matte knife, then staple, hot glue, or white glue them together to make a weblike grid. The vertical strips determine the height of the scenery, while the horizontal strips refine the contours. The strip method is flexible: If a mountain is too tall it can be crushed down and held there with a strip of cardboard and a dab of glue. If you don't like a section of scenery, just cut it away and replace it. I cover the cardboard strips with plaster-impregnated gauze (Rigid Wrap) or plaster-soaked paper towels.

Styrofoam insulation. Common extruded Styrofoam insulation sheet has become a popular scenic base in the last 20 years. It comes in sheets 2' wide by 8' long in 1" and 2" thicknesses. Glue it into stacks, then shape it with a serrated knife, hacksaw blades, and coarse rasps (the chief drawback is the sheer volume of messy chaff that you generate). Styrofoam can be textured directly with latex paint and ground foam, or first covered with plaster, Rigid Wrap, or Sculptamold.

COMMON SCENERY PLASTERS

Someone always asks "can I use plaster of Paris instead of Hydrocal," or "what's the difference between molding plaster and Gypsolite?" Here's a rundown of the most popular scenery plasters. (There are probably more types of plaster available than there are types of model trees. The plasters are graded and the specifications written to satisfy the demands of engineers and scientists, not modelers. The bottom line is that they all can make great scenery!)

Molding plaster was formulated for casting. Its texture is very fine, thus producing sharp, clean castings, and it sets in about 10 minutes. Molding plaster expands as it sets, forcing itself into the mold. Compared to other plasters it's relatively soft and absorbs a lot of paint.

Plaster of Paris is the workhorse of model railroad scenery building because it's readily available. It's cheap, sets slower than molding plaster, and is harder, so it requires several applications of thinned paint to color it.

Hydrocal used to be the darling of the zip-texturing crowd because it's strong, hard, and sets in about 10 minutes. The term "hardshell" was coined to describe the unique properties of Hydrocal. It's not available everywhere, but similar high-strength plasters can be substituted for it.

GYPSOLITE AS A SCENERY SHELL MATERIAL

A relatively new material on the scenery front is Gypsolite. I used it to make a strong, lightweight scenery shell on the HO scale Pennsylvania Railroad that I built for *Model Railroader* magazine.

Gypsolite is called a base-coat plaster because masons use it as the first coat when plastering the walls of a house. It has a lot of the characteristics of cement: slow setting time, up to one hour of working time, lots of realistic texture, and high strength —

it's stronger than Hydrocal. Gypsolite is filled with perlite, little balls of expanded mica. It takes paint well, absorbing color to blend exactly with rock castings. You'll find it at large masonry suppliers.

I trowel a ¼" layer of Gypsolite over the scenery shell. The Gypsolite seals and hardens the shell and provides tooth to help hold the scenic foam. It's also the perfect medium to hold rock castings on the scenic base. I've used rock castings with very thin cross-sections, applied using Gypsolite as the glue. Wet the surface where the casting will go and trowel on a 1/2"-thick layer. Dip each casting in water to wet it and butter 1/8" of Gypsolite on the back. Push the thin castings into place, arranging them realistically. If Gypsolite oozes from between the castings, smooth or remove it with a wet brush.

TINKERING WITH PLASTER SETTING TIMES

I recommend strongly against doing so, but somebody always wants to know how to alter the setting time of plaster or Hydrocal. All molding and Hydrocal-type plasters are formulated to have documented working times, hardness, and strength when used following the manufacturer's recommendations. Anything other than pure water added to the plaster will increase or retard the setting time, change its working characteristics, or weaken it.

Experimentation is the key. Mix small trial batches of plaster with measured amounts of whatever it is you want to add, then document the results.

Mix **standard plaster** by adding 2 cups of plaster to 1 cup of cold water. Pour in the plaster slowly and let the water absorb it, then stir thoroughly.

To **prolong** the working time add 1 teaspoon (more or less, experiment!) of vinegar.

To **accelerate** setting time add 1/2 teaspoon of table salt.

SCULPTING MIX FOR LIGHTWEIGHT SCENERY

In the December 1993 issue of *Model Railroader* Lou Sassi wrote about his secret goop for covering Styrofoam scenery. This papier-mache-like stuff is easy to work, dries strong, and is lightweight. Try it!

Lou's recipe:

1 cup Perma-Scene
1 cup Celluclay
1/4-1/3 cup white glue

STRONGER SCULPTAMOLD

Sculptamold Modeling Compound is an American Art Clay Company product with working properties similar to plaster. After setting it's strong and lightweight, and it takes paints and stains much like plaster.

Sculptamold has long been a favorite scenery material for model railroads because it's easy to work with and easy to clean up, and has great texture. I've used it for every type of scenery project: to build hills and roads, make rocks, and contour around structures. It mixes with water, sets in about

20 minutes, and dries overnight to make strong, lightweight scenery.

Sculptamold is satisfactory when mixed as directed, but I've experimented with several ways to make it a bit harder and stronger. The best recipe I've found is to add white glue to the water.

Put 1 cup of Sculptamold in a mixing bowl and add 1/2 cup of diluted white glue (3 parts water to 1 part white glue). Mix this thoroughly with a spatula and spread some on a scrap piece of Styrofoam for a test. (More or less liquid can be added to obtain the consistency you like.) You'll find that it sticks to the Styrofoam better and can be spread thin without lifting or curling. It takes textures well and can be smoothed with a wet brush. Try this mixture to make a blacktop road — it's easier to work than standard Sculptamold.

COLORING SCULPTAMOLD WITH EARTH-TONE LATEX PAINT

Coloring agents can be added to Sculptamold without noticeably changing its working characteristics. I like to substitute diluted latex paint for water.

Here's a good formula to start with:

Mix 1 quart of earth-colored latex paint with 1 quart of water. (This is the same mixture that will be used to paint the rest of your scenery.)

Mix 1 cup of Sculptamold and 1/2 cup of the diluted earth paint.

Trowel this mixture over a Styrofoam or other scenery base. It can be smoothed with a wet palette

knife or with your fingers to achieve the surface texture you like. This mixture is especially useful for portable layouts, scenery edges and corners, or high-wear areas. Also try it for setting structures in place (you don't have to paint so closely around them), and for other places where it's hard to paint. I always use this mixture around bridge abutments and footings.

FLAT-BACKED SCULPTAMOLD BOULDERS

I can't bring myself to throw away extra Sculpta-mold. When I have a few gobs left over, I throw them down on a scrap of waxed paper, manipulate them briefly to make them look like protruding boulders, and let them dry.

Paint the boulders with earth paint, shade and

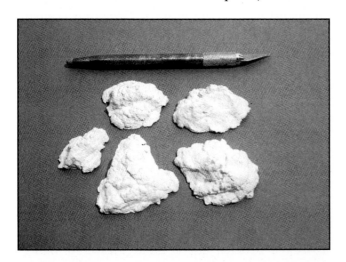

color them like rock castings, and drop them into place in stream beds or as boulders to break up open grassy surfaces. They look great — and they're free!

BUILDING FOAM SCENERY

Malcolm Furlow pioneered the use of expanded foam scenery on the HOn3 San Juan Central layout that he built for *Model Railroader*. Now many professionals as well as amateur builders use it exclusively as a base for their scenery. It's lightweight, flexible, and strong. It can be laminated and shaped, and almost any scenery building method can be used on top of it.

There are two types of plastic foam in common use. The easier to obtain and use is sheet Styrofoam. Two types are available: white bead board, 1" thick in 2' x 6' sheets; and Dow-Corning blue (or pink,

depending on the fire rating) extruded Styrofoam insulating sheet in 2' x 8' sheets in thicknesses ranging from ³/₄" to 3".

The second type of scenery foam is available from Mountains in Minutes. It's a two-part polyfoam that you mix, then pour over the scenery support, where it expands. Two-part polyfoam is used by many professionals with an electric-pump spray nozzle to direct the foam.

The down side of either type of foam is that it's messy and effected by petroleum-based solvents. The fine powder that's generated when foam is cut or shaped sticks to everything! During shaping operations I work with a vacuum cleaner hose in one hand, sucking the foam dust away before it's released into the air. All adhesives and paints used with foam

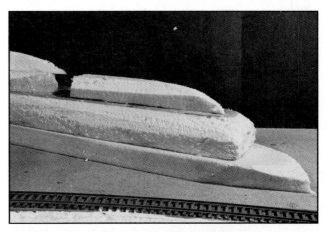

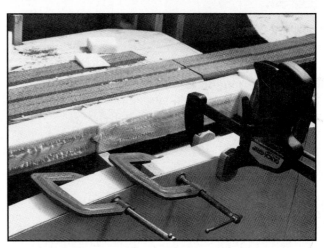

must be water-based — no exceptions!

Scenic contours can be built up in layers from pieces cut from the Styrofoam sheets. The stack is held together with a Styrofoam-compatible adhesive such as Liquid Nails (a common construction adhesive), white glue, or water-soluble mastic. Texture paint or Sculptamold can be used to fill holes, cracks and seams, and to refine the rough contours.

Rocks can be cast over the Styrofoam base using two-part Mountains in Minutes polyfoam castings or traditional plaster techniques. For polyfoam, the molds are coated with plenty of mold release agent (I use Armor-All or Scotchguard in spray cans), allowed to dry, then filled with a mixture of resin and catalyst. When the foam begins to expand, hold the mold in place over the scenery base until the foam hardens. The molds can also be filled with foam and set aside to cure. Then the rock castings are trimmed and glued onto the scenery.

If you're using plaster in rubber molds, just fill the molds with stiff plaster and push in place over the base. Hold the mold until the plaster sets, then peel it away. Rock faces can also be produced on the workbench by filling the molds and letting the plaster set. The finished rocks are glued to the Styrofoam base and painted.

CHEMICAL CARVING FOR STYROFOAM

While admiring the beautiful carved Styrofoam bridges on Clark Dunham's newest display, "America's Railroads on Parade," I asked how they were made. My attempts at carving Styrofoam had always been disappointing, because it's a hard material to cut cleanly. Clark's rocks and stones were clean, crisp, and loaded with detail, and he told me the secret was a solution of acetone and water.

The technique is simple: You need only carving tools, acetone, and water in a spray bottle. Carve the Styrofoam with knives or other tools until it looks like rock or stone, then add surface texture using a hacksaw blade or wire brush.

Now for the chemical carving. Be sure to work with plenty of ventilation, and don't smoke or allow an open flame in the vicinity. Brush on acetone, working in a small area and watching closely. The acetone will smooth, soften, and dissolve the foam. When the etching almost reaches the point where you say "enough," spray the area with water. This will dilute the acetone, stop the etching, and wash away the excess.

Repeat the sequence on the rest of carving; the process is controllable, and you can work on small areas. The only trick is to watch what's happening and stop it before it goes too far.

After the water spray, the foam will be soft and spongy. You can let the water dry and the surface harden, or add more texture. The easiest texture is obtained by beating the foam with the wire brush, leaving a pebbled effect. Make strata by lightly dragging a saw blade over the foam surface.

Experiment with chemical carving and you'll discover other variations on the technique. Try shaping the Styrofoam with a heat gun before the acetone application. One last word of caution — be careful with all solvents around Styrofoam. While writing this tip I set a jar of mineral spirits (paint thinner) on a Styrofoam scenery section; just minutes later the jar had partially disappeared into the terrain.

BUILDING STYROFOAM LIFTOUTS

An awful lot of needless worry has been lavished on making "invisible" liftout hatches to cover access holes. The simple truth is that they're easy to make, and a lot easier to disguise than most folks think they'll be.

You can make liftouts from just about anything, including the materials you choose for the rest of your scenic shell. I like extruded Styrofoam insulation board best because of its combination of lightness and resilience. Cut the parts to the rough contours of the liftout, then assemble them with 5-minute epoxy or Liquid Nails construction adhesive. Larger liftouts need extra 1" x 2" Styrofoam braces to strengthen the bottom, and you should add handles

where appropriate. (You can even put a handle on top of the liftout if there will be a removable building to cover it.)

When the rough liftout is done and you're sure it fits in the corresponding hole in the railroad, pull it out and form the Styrofoam terrain to the final contours. I like to do this outdoors or over a trash can so cleanup isn't such a chore. Paint the foam base with earth-colored latex paint, then add texture and

matte medium bonding spray and allow to dry overnight.

WORKING A LIFTOUT INTO YOUR RAILROAD

When the basic form of the liftout is complete and dry, test-fit it into the hole in the layout. If more material needs to be shaved off the contours, do it now, then paint and add more texture. If some contours need to be built up, don't worry about that until the next step.

Line the hole in the layout with plastic food wrap film, then fit the liftout. Work the film out over the layout for an inch or two from the hatch. Mix small batches of reinforced Sculptamold scenery compound (use a 50-50 water and white glue solution instead of water), and use it to feather edges on the hatch so they overlap the layout scenery. The overlap should be $1/4$" to $1/2$" out from the edges of the liftout.

Let the Sculptamold dry overnight, maybe more, then carefully pry the liftout hatch out of the layout. Paint and texture the new edges, let dry again, then test fit the hatch in the layout one more time.

By now the edges of the liftout should be pretty hard to see, and disguising them further is easy. Make small applications of texture that overlap the edges, being sure to pry up the hatch so the bonding solution can't glue it into the layout. For those few tough spots, try covering them with a pinches of loose texture and simply replacing it when the hatch has to be removed.

After all the worry expended on them, once they're built it turns out that most liftouts aren't removed more than a couple of times a year, if even that often.

PAINT COLORS FOR SCENERY

Every time I start a new layout or diorama the first thing I do is select colors for earth — with light and dark variations — rocks, mud or wet earth, and blue sky. These colors are important because they help identify the locale of the railroad.

I visit the area if possible to gather earth and rock samples; if this is not possible I study color slides. The next step is to take my samples to the paint store and look through the color chips until I find a close match. I have the store mix a quart of flat interior latex of each color.

Some good starting points if you're modeling the Northeast:

Basic earth color. In a large plastic bottle mix one quart of Pittsburgh No. 3610 Poplar with one quart wet water.

Light earth color. Mix 1 part basic earth color to 1 part flat white and few drops of wetting agent.

Basic rock color. Mix 1 part basic earth color with 3 parts wet water.

Also mix a small amount of **Basic dark earth** color, Pittsburgh No. 7605 Tortoise, with equal parts wet water. Use this for freshly plowed areas, wet soil, and around ponds and streams.

Sky blue. I like Sears Easy Living No. 223, Bluejay, or Sears No. SCCS 762, Royal Blue Medium Bright. Use the sky blue, straight from the can, at the top of the backdrop and gradually add more flat white as you approach the horizon.

BLACK WASH I

I usually use some kind of black wash on all my models after the initial color is applied. This tones down and dirties all painted surfaces, and after the wash dries I follow up by dry-brushing with off

white. This light-over-dark combination amplifies surface texture and lightly weathers the model.

I choose one of three different black washes depending upon the surface or modeling material. My first formula, developed more than 20 years ago, was based on black pigmented wiping stain, which is lampblack pigment suspended in linseed oil. I dilute about 1 teaspoon of lampblack in a pint of odorless mineral spirits paint thinner. Flow this wash onto painted plastic, wood, and plaster models. The paint thinner has a very low surface tension, which helps the black to flow into cracks and crevices, darkening them.

BLACK WASH II

Make a water-soluble black wash from black universal tinting color, available in paint stores. Mix about a 2"-long squiggle (it comes in a tube) of black in a pint of wet water (tap water to which several drops of dishwashing detergent or Kodak Photo-Flo wetting agent have been added). Use this for structures, figures, vehicles, or anywhere a thinner-based wash might soften the underlying paint coat. It doesn't flow as readily as a mineral-spirits wash, but with care you can achieve excellent results with it.

BLACK WASH III

The wash I use most for scenery is made from 1 teaspoon of black India ink in a pint of rubbing alcohol. I flow this mixture over roads, gravel piles, fences, and rocks. It's especially good for painting shadows on rock faces, and it can be substituted for either of the washes mentioned above.

One important warning for using any black wash:

Don't overdo it — a little goes a long way! Experiment first so you can gauge the results, and remember that it's better (and easier!) to slowly build up the effect you want with repeated applications of a thin wash than it is to remove a heavy wash that's turned out too dark.

DULLING POLLY S FOR SCENERY

Every so often when I apply Polly S flat paint over a smooth plaster or Hydrocal surface, it will dry with more sheen than I'd like. One solution is to mix a little talcum powder with the paint before brushing. You'll have to experiment to determine exact proportions.

Combine 3 teaspoons of paint with about 1/2 teaspoon of unscented talcum powder in a shallow dish. If the paint thickens, mix in several drops of water. The powder may alter the color slightly, so test it on a piece of scrap wood or plaster before using it on scenery.

EVEN WETTER WATER

The usual formula for wet water consists of a few drops of dishwashing detergent in a quart of water, and a few drops of Kodak Photo-Flo works better yet. For those jobs where you need a solution with even less surface tension, try adding a tablespoon or two of isopropyl alcohol (rubbing alcohol) to the sprayer. The alcohol will reduce the surface tension of the water to the absolute minimum, and make jobs like ballasting a lot easier.

EXTRA-FINE SPRAYERS FOR SCENERY

For most scenery jobs a standard household sprayer is the best tool, and many of them even provide a choice between fine and coarse sprays. But when it comes to spraying small areas with wet water solution or matte medium bonding spray, nothing beats the fine spray provided by the pump spray head that comes on non-aerosol hair spray.

You can leave the wet water spray in the bottle as long as you want, but it's important to empty out the bonding spray and clean the pump and spray head after every use; otherwise the pump will be glued solid. I also make it a practice to strain the diluted matte medium through a fine tea strainer before I use it. The fine sprayer is perfect for adding a little ground foam around a structure base, or for sprucing up an old scene with a few touches of bright new texture.

RUBBER ROCKS

I started making rubber rocks to protect the edges of a portable layout from bumps and bruises, and to soften the blows resulting from moving the layout. If

you know how to make a regular latex rock mold then you can make rubber rocks: Rubber rocks are positives and rock molds are negatives.

In addition to a rock master and liquid latex molding compound you'll need Flexwax, a low-melt-ing-point (120° F.) wax for making three-dimensional molds. It can be remelted and used over and over again. I found a 2½-pound block of it in the same craft store that sold me the latex molding compound.

The process is easy: Melt Flexwax and brush it on the surface of your rock. Build up several layers so the mold will not tear when it's removed. While the mold is still warm remove it from the rock and put it in the refrigerator for about 30 minutes to firm it up. Now brush five or six layers of liquid latex molding compound into the Flexwax mold. Add cheesecloth for strength between the fourth and fifth layers.

After the latex dries remove it from the mold, trim, and paint to look like the rest of the rocks on your layout. I set the rocks on a sheet of newspaper in a well-ventilated area and spray them with Krylon Leather Brown. While they are still wet I spray a shadow color using Krylon Flat Black. Aim the spray can pointing upward so the black coats only the undersides of protruding faces. When dry, mist the rocks with Floquil Earth to highlight the top surfaces of rocks, then finish by dry-brushing highlights with Polly S Reefer White.

Rubber rocks can be glued to the scenic base with Liquid Nails. Just run a bead around the inside edge of each rock and push it into place.

PAVEMENT CRACKS AND PATCHES

Add realism to your roads by simulating tar repairs to cracks and making different, usually

darker-colored, areas to represent places where the street has been dug up and repaired. You can do all this with paint. I like Mars Black acrylic right out of the tube for tar strips, and a good way to apply it is with a plastic syringe made for applying wood glue. Make patches by drawing a rectangle on the pavement and brush painting dark gray repaired areas.

MODELING HOT-TOP ROADS

Hot top (also called bituminous, tarmac, macadam, or blacktop) roads can be quickly and effectively modeled. The base I use is $^3/_{16}$" thick Fome-cor board cut to the correct width and glued in place on the scenery support with Liquid Nails. After gluing down the board I work the scenery up to the edges and seal it with a coat of basic earth color.

After the paint dries, brush white glue on the road

surface and sprinkle fine sand through a tea strainer (a folded piece of nylon stocking can be used instead) into the glue. Add enough sand to cover the surface of the road completely (excess can be vacuumed after the glue dries).

To make the surface look like hot top, mix 3 parts flat black latex paint, 2 parts white, 1 part raw sienna, and enough water to double the volume. Brush a thick layer over the sifted sand. This mixture separates into its individual colors on the road surface, rendering it less regular and more weathered.

After paint dries, weather the road with a wash made from 2 parts Polly S Flat Black and 3 parts Polly S Concrete diluted with 5 parts wet water. Apply several similar washes, some lighter, some darker, to make the road look patched and repaired. Finish by adding fresh tar seams and patches with a fine-tip black marking pen.

CARVING DURHAM'S WATER PUTTY

Durham's Rock Hard Water Putty is a plasterlike material that's an old standby for modeling stone walls and brick or cobblestone streets. What most folks don't know is that you can repeatedly re-wet the dried material and continue carving detail into it. Moisten the surface of the dried Durham's with a solution of lukewarm water and liquid hand soap, let it sit for a minute or two, then go to work carving in

detail and texture with dental tools or hobby knives.

TRICKS WITH TUNNEL PORTALS

Tunnel portals are the first scenery items you should add to your layout. They should be in place and tunnel interiors finished soon after your track is down, because if you wait until after the scenic shell is built you won't be able to paint and detail inside the tunnel.

I like the Chooch assortment of HO tunnel entrances. Paint them with Floquil Concrete and weather them with black wash. Dry-brush the portals with Polly S Reefer White using a stiff brush, and finish weathering with pastel chalks. After the

scenery is built I airbrush flat black onto the front of the portals to simulate decades of smoke.

Set each portal in place, raising the bottom with squares of cork roadbed until even with the track

height. I fasten them with a dab of Liquid Nails on the bottom of each portal leg. Keep the portal upright and perpendicular to the track with blocks of wood and small weights until the adhesive dries.

After ballasting the track several inches into each tunnel entrance, model the inside walls of the portals by installing flat pieces of prepainted and weathered cast stone. Position the stone sheets to prevent viewers from seeing the benchwork when looking into the tunnel. Mask the track and spray flat black paint on any visible benchwork.

Before starting your scenic shell, glue cardboard wings behind each tunnel portal for attaching cardboard strips. These keep the strips from interfering with the portal or getting in the way of your trains.

BRIDGE ABUTMENTS

The easiest bridge abutments to paint and install are the polyurethane castings made by Chooch. I build, paint, and weather the bridge first. Then I establish the correct vertical position for the bridge by laying a steel straightedge on the ties at each end of the bridge gap. With the straightedge flat on the ties at both ends, draw location marks at each end.

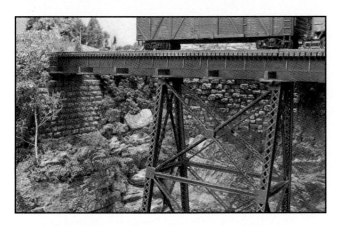

Prepare the abutments by painting and weathering them. Squeeze a bead of Liquid Nails on the back of each abutment and push it into place using the location marks. Set the bridge on the abutments, lay the straightedge back on the ties, and push the abutments up or down to adjust. Space left under the abutments can be filled with small stripwood shims before the adhesive hardens.

I do all this before the scenery is in place. When adding rock castings, sand or file each casting edge so that it will butt to the abutment to make the smallest seam possible. Fill unsightly gaps with grass or foliage material.

MAKING CURVED RETAINING WALLS

Model railroads squeeze as much track as pos-

sible into a given space, and that usually means using retaining walls. All the walls I've seen offered are flat, but often a curved wall would look more realistic and better utilize tight quarters.

Here are two ways to curve flat walls. The first works with polyurethane walls like those from Chooch. Set your oven on low (170° F.) and place the casting in the oven for 30 to 40 minutes. This will soften it enough to bend it into a curve.

The second method involves using a rubber mold. Some manufacturers, including Mountains in Minutes, encourage modelers to make latex molds of their walls and rocks. In fact, they even sell all the stuff you'll need to do it. Make a mold of your favorite wall, fill the mold with plaster, set it over a curved surface (like a peanut butter jar), and hold the ends in place until the plaster sets. Carefully remove the casting and check the curve. If it's too sharp or too shallow, just use a different jar.

CUSTOM ABUTMENTS FROM PLASTER WALL CASTINGS

Another good source of realistic bridge abutments is retaining wall castings, either plastic or plaster. I've made a number of molds to make plaster retaining walls, and the castings are easy to cut up to fit beneath a bridge (a bandsaw makes quick work of cutting them up, but the plaster wrecks the blade).

REALISTIC CEMENT-BLOCK WALLS

Pete Laier showed me yet another source of scratchbuilding materials. These are 1/35 scale Tamiya interlocking brick wall sections made for

military modelers. The brick pieces are made of styrene and can be joined with liquid plastic cement. When painted gray the brick wall pieces look about the right size for HO cement blocks. Pete uses them to build block foundations and small outbuildings around his industrial pike.

Dick Patterson's layout features hundreds of miniature pines and unique removable trees.

2
Tips for texture and trees

Growing things to make your scenery look like the real world

TRAINS AND TRACKS are harsh, hard, mechanical things, but they operate in a world of lush vegetation. Even western mountain railroads roll through scenes with a surprising number of trees and bushes, and I have yet to see a model railroad that has enough trees.

Today's hobby shops offer a wonderful variety of tree kits and scenic texture materials to green up

your layout. Here are tips and techniques for making the most of this cornucopia of colors and textures.

CHOOSING STANDARD FOAM COLORS

When you're planning the scenery on your railroad or thinking about refurbishing it, consider selecting standard foam colors. The idea is to establish a palette of greens, browns, golds, and reds that you'll use as the basic scenery texture. I buy many different foam shades and mix them until I have several pleasing combinations. I keep a record what's in each mixture so it can be duplicated.

Plastic supermarket bags are ideal for storing the blended colors. A typical foam formula is about 80 percent coarse and 20 percent fine foam (a combination of three shades of green, two shades of brown, and a gold-yellow). These mixtures are used to make background trees and cover hills and fields. For foreground scenery and around structures I use the same basic combinations but add more fine foam to the blend.

USING SAWDUST TEXTURE

Older modelers remember when the only scenery textures were bright-green sawdust grass and chocolate-brown sawdust earth. Today we've got lots of

better textures — especially ground foam — and sawdust is almost forgotten.

But dyed sawdust has a texture that's unique. When glued on the scenic base and colored properly, it can look like tall grass, leaves, heavy brush, or dense undergrowth. It also makes a great sub-texture for foam. Lightly sprinkling scenic foam over a base of dyed sawdust provides three-dimensional relief, because of the contrast of fine texture over coarse.

Complete instructions for dyeing sawdust are in *How to Build Realistic Model Railroad Scenery*, published by Kalmbach.

REAL DIRT TEXTURE

Some folks swear by real dirt, sand, and decomposed granite to make absolutely the best simulation of earth and rocks on their model railroads. I like it too, because it's another useful weapon in my arsenal of scenery textures.

Every place I go I gather several coffee cans of the local dirt. When I get home I spread each can on several thicknesses of newspaper to dry. Several days later I sift the dirt through a piece of $\frac{1}{4}$"-mesh

screen to remove larger stones and organic matter. I screen it again through an old window screen to separate it into two grades, coarse and fine.

Next is the most important step: Run a strong magnet through the different grades of dirt. This removes metal particles that would eventually work their way into your locomotive motors.

To apply, paint on white glue diluted with an

equal amount of water and sprinkle the dirt over it. Piles of dirt and stones can be arranged around the scenery using a soft brush, and held in place with a squirt of wet water followed by dilute white glue applied with an eyedropper.

A DRINKING STRAW FOR DISPENSING SCENIC TEXTURE

Shaker jars are great for applying the initial texture to broad areas, but once the scenery is roughed out, I often need a way to dispense smaller volumes of fine texture, especially sand, around structures and other tight areas.

When the shaker jar is too big and distributing texture by the pinch — the amount you can trap between your thumb and forefinger — will take too long, try loading up about half a plastic drinking straw with texture. Then hold the tip of the straw where you need the texture and lightly tap the side to dispense exactly the amounts you need — and exactly where you want them.

FINE SAND FOR TOUCHING UP

Real scenery doesn't have much in the way of hard edges between, say, grass and bare earth, and I often come up with unrealistic raw edges beside the track or along the sides of the road. It's easy to use common fine beach sand or mineral texture to touch up such edges.

Moisten the edge you want to disguise with wet water, then dribble on dilute matte medium bonding solution. Then use your forefinger and thumb to dispense pinches of sand exactly where needed to cover up the rough area. Use pinches of ballast to touch up at trackside, and finish with more matte medium bonding solution.

PAINTING SAND OR BALLAST

It doesn't happen often, but once in a while a scenic texture just won't look right after application. Sand can turn out sort of translucent, or not the right color. Sand and ballast can be tinted with stains,

washes, or dry-brushed to render them the characteristic color and tone for the railroad or region that you're modeling.

I learned this trick from the military diorama modelers, who paint everything, whether it's the right color or not, and it's a good technique to have up your sleeve.

FLOCKING — A BREAK
FROM SCENIC FOAM

Nothing looks better in foreground scenes than little blades of grass all standing at attention. The best foreground grass is made with flocking, also called static grass. It's applied by putting it in a spice jar (with holes in the lid) and shaking it over scenery moistened with diluted matte medium.

I apply the flocking over a base coat of medium

green scenic foam. It'll stick and cover in a thick layer and looks like long grass because it's the right color. Flocking is available from Express Model Landscaping (see Addresses) in a wide variety of colors and sizes.

A new invention, a plastic squeeze bottle with a piece of soft-rubber magnet wrapped around the neck, is being offered as an applicator. The magnet charges the flocking particles as they leave the bottle.

Fill the bottle with static grass, pop on the top, and squeeze. If you're close enough to the scenery and use enough force most of the flocking will land standing up.

MODELING A DAISY FIELD

If you're in a rut and want to spice up your scenery, try creating a daisy field. Not only will it draw attention to itself, but it will brighten its surroundings, adding color to the overall scene.

First you need a field, any open area covered with

green scenic foam. Spray the field with wet water followed by a second spraying of diluted matte medium (1 part matte medium to 3 parts water). Over the wet area I sprinkle yellow punched-paper "leaves." (One brand is offered by K&S Scenery; see Addresses in the back of this book.) You could also use yellow scenic foam, applied with a shaker jar.

After the matte medium dries, vacuum away excess daisies — and enjoy.

MAKING STRING WEEDS

All kinds of realistic weeds can be made from plain string. I like package twine, the coarse brown furry stuff called sisal. If you can't find it, try boiling white "corned beef" string in water for several minutes to eliminate the sizing, then drain.

To dye the string, boil a cup of water in an old pot and add several tablespoons of green fabric dye. Dissolve the dye, then soak the string for 10 to 15 minutes until it absorbs the color. Darken the color by adding more dye to the water. Remove the string from the pot and hang it up to dry. Add a wood spring-type clothespin to the lower end so that the string will dry straight.

To use, cut the string into short lengths, dip the ends in white glue, and insert them in pre-drilled holes in the scenic base. After the glue dries use your finger or the tip of an X-acto knife to spread and fluff the weed top. Trim to different lengths with scissors. Thin, scraggly looking weeds can be made by drag-

ging a fine-toothed comb through the weeds to remove loose fibers.

Model cattails and flowering weeds by gluing scenic foam to the tops of the weeds. If you want to change the color or add colorful variety to the weeds, stroke them with various colored felt markers. Common water-soluble markers can be found in art and craft stores in shades just right for coloring vegetation.

MODELING TALL GRASS

Fake fur, low pile indoor-outdoor carpeting, and even old terrycloth towels can be used to model tall grass. These materials can be found at fabric stores or anywhere cloth remnants are sold.

A piece about two feet square will go a long way on a model railroad. If you use fake fur choose a fabric with ½" pile that has a fairly stiff texture. I cut a

piece to fit over the scenery base, brush the base with full-strength white glue, and push the grass in place. Set small weights or push pins around the edges to hold the fabric down until the glue dries. The edges will have a tendency to curl upward. (Do not push on the weights or the glue will be squeezed up through

the fabric into the nap, causing it to mat.) After the glue dries at least overnight, carefully remove the pins or weights.

Trim away loose edges with scissors, then run a comb through the grass to remove loose hairs or threads. To color the grass use a thin stain and flow it on with a wide brush. Floquil R-36 Weyerhauser Green looks good when thinly applied over light-colored fake fur.

The coloring technique involves brushing the wash onto a 6"-square area. If the color looks too dark, pick up a brushload of thinner and scrub it into the painted area. Other green tints or earth colors can be dappled into the grass for variety. Allow the paint to dry for several days, then fluff the nap with a stiff brush.

Thin spots in the grass can be covered with bits of lichen or other foliage, or sprinkled with sifted earth. Use extra scenic foam around the edges to blend the tall grass into the adjacent scenery.

LEAVES AROUND YOUR STRUCTURES

One of the little details that will tie your struc-

tures to the scenery is an accumulation of dead leaves. These can be modeled from brownish-tan sawdust or scenic foam. Sprinkle a pinch around the structure, push the dead leaves up against the building (or anywhere wind would deposit them) with a soft brush, and make them permanent with several drops of diluted matte medium.

This is the type of detail that your visitors don't really notice, but without the leaves your buildings will look as though they were just plunked down on top of the scenery. You could call the leaves "subliminal detail."

SCENIC FIBER AND FOAM BUSHES

Woodland Scenics Green Poly Fiber material is a great substitute for lichen for background scenery. I first experimented with it because quality lichen became hard to come by a few years back.

To make tree balls, take a bag of Green Poly Fiber and stretch it into thin, wispy chunks. Keep pulling the fiber to make it as thin as possible — the thinner you make it, the better the finished tree balls will look. As I stretch the fiber I tear off a piece and roll it into a ball before tossing it into a shallow pan of matte medium diluted 4:1 with water. Plan on getting between 50 and 60 golf-ball-sized pieces per bag. I wear rubber gloves to give me more traction and keep my hands clean.

After all the fiber balls are in the container of matte medium, grab a handful and squeeze out excess liquid. Toss them into a bag of coarse scenic foam. You'll want to use several shades of green plus at least one brown foam; I fill half a dozen plastic supermarket shopping bags with enough foam in

different colors to make about a thousand fiber balls at a time.

Coat the balls with foam and arrange them on waxed paper to dry. Plant them by dipping in diluted white glue and setting them close together on your scenic base.

SCULPEY FOR MAKING STUMPS

Sculpey is a white claylike material sold in hobby and crafts stores for sculpting and carving. After shaping it can be permanently hardened by baking. The hardened material takes on many of the characteristics of ceramic.

I use Sculpey to make stumps for logging areas. I

carve small balls of Sculpey into stumps with the tip of a hobby knife, dental tool, or toothpick. The carving is done on a smooth, heat-resistant surface like plywood, glass, or plexiglass. After the stumps are baked I remove them from the base, paint them with acrylics, and glue them to the layout.

When a lot of stumps are needed I carve a dozen different types and sizes, bake, then glue them in a tight group on a piece of styrene. The stumps are coated with several layers of liquid latex rubber to make a mold similar to a rock mold. Hundreds of plaster stump replicas can be made from one mold; in fact, I have yet to wear out a stump mold!

DEAD TREES AND DEAD WOOD

Several great materials are available to

model dead wood and trees, and they're all free! I use natural weeds gathered in the winter, sagebrush branches, sumac tips, and even garden trimmings. A pleasant hour or so spent in your backyard, a city park, or along the highway will yield all sorts of interesting dead-wood details. I also save all the trimmings from tree-making projects and use them to model piles of firewood beside rural structures.

Cut the wood pieces into short lengths with wire cutters and store in plastic bags. To make interest-

ing clutter group the dead wood in small piles; try to include several sizes and shapes piled in a haphazard manner. Hold the wood in place with white glue or matte medium.

MODELING SNAGS

Snags — uprooted stumps and whole trees that have been swept away by flood waters — are found in and around moving water, or where stumps get uprooted by heavy rain, mud slides, or logging.

Western modelers will want to use gnarled pieces of sagebrush, and eastern folks should look for weeds, roots, and small branches that have a lot of bark detail. I cut forking and branching sections from the middle of the twigs. The best description of

what part to cut is to use the analogy of your wrist, hand and fingers. Find a piece that has a straight stem with lots of small branches at its base. The stem is the wrist, where the branching begins is the hand, and all the small branches are the fingers. Cut the twig about $1/4$" to $1/2$" from the hand, on the wrist. Cut the branches (fingers) to many different lengths, from $1/4$" to $3/4$" long. Make them all different sizes.

Lightly dry-brush each snag with flat white to accent the bark detail and to give it a bleached, weathered look. Glue the snags on their sides, or in a tangle at the edge or middle of a body of water.

SAVING READY-MADE TREES

Inexpensive ready-made trees can help bulk out the forests on your layout. Start by vigorously bending all the branches downward until they are almost horizontal. Don't worry if some of the foam falls off, we're going to add more later. The idea is to do away with the "tulip" look where all the branches point skyward at about the same angle. For variety, re-

move several of the interior branches of the tree before applying glue and foam. This breaks up the machine-made symmetry.

Next, mount the trees on a sheet of scrap cardboard or Styrofoam and give them a drenching with diluted white glue (3 parts water to 1 part white

glue) from a household sprayer bottle. Sprinkle on a couple of colors of coarse green ground foam and remove the excess by shaking the trees in a plastic bag. The coarse foam bulks out the trees and gives them a nice shape.

If the trees already have a good shape and you just want to add another interesting texture, try sprinkling punched-paper "leaves" over the glue. These are available from several scenery sources. The best selection is from Express Model Landscaping Supplies.

These trees look best when grouped with homemade weed trees and other kit-built trees. They provide anonymous bulk and general tree texture for your forests.

TIPS FOR TREE KITS

Suppose you've got a tree kit that makes six trees, and you've got the trunks and branches all set up and are ready to add the foliage material. Before you do anything else, take the foliage material and cut it into six approximately equal sections. This ensures that you won't run out of foliage after the third tree!

When stretching the foliage material before attaching it to the armature, stretch it as much as you think the instructions call for, then stretch it some more. The more you stretch, the better the tree will look — we're after that see-through look, after all — and I've never met anybody who had the patience to overdo it. So keep stretching!

When applying the foam foliage over the netting, it's best to make two applications of adhesive and foam. Allow an overnight drying period in between. Work over clean newspapers so the foam or foliage that doesn't stick to the tree can be retrieved and reused on other trees or elsewhere on your layout.

It's best to use at least two different colors of foam on every tree. Try sprinkling on dark green foam with the tree held upside down, then medium or light green with the tree upright. This builds a light-and-shadow look. Sometimes you can even add a third color like light yellow-green to simulate sunlight striking only the tops of leaves.

Try a little pruning on trees before installing them on the layout to ensure there are no unrealistic stray branches sticking out at right angles to the rest of the tree shape. Don't manicure them, though!

WOODLAND SCENICS TREES

I remove the stubby mounting pin from the bottom of the trunk of cast-metal Woodland Scenics

tree kits, file the bottom flat, and drill a hole into the trunk with a No. 62 drill. Then I glue in a 1½" length of 1/32" brass wire. This longer, thinner pin serves as a good handle for holding the tree, makes it easy to poke the tree into a Styrofoam block, and simplifies installing the tree on the layout.

TREE-PLANTING TRICKS

Three simple tricks can go a long way toward adding variety and realism to your scale forests:

First, if trees come with relatively long trunks, cut off varying lengths to make the finished trees of differing heights.

Second, one large tree can provide enough material for two or three smaller ones — or dozens of bushes.

Third, many trees based on a natural foliage growth or dried weeds can be improved by bending the branches further out from the main stem when planting. Don't be afraid of breaking the branch; if you do, it will either be supported by the surrounding branches, or it will become one of those smaller trees you were planning to plant anyhow.

SMOKE-BUSH TREE ARMATURES

Weed stems make excellent tree armatures, particularly when you need a lot of them. The dried flowers of the smoke bush are available from several scenery distributors, or you can buy a smoke bush plant from a garden center or mail-order catalog and grow your own. I had a smoke bush in my yard for

many years, and enjoyed free trees until an infestation of aphids ate it one year.

These dried flowers make realistic trees either by themselves or in clusters. Smoke bush armatures are available from Express Model Landscaping Supplies.

LEAVES FOR SMOKE-BUSH TREES

The dried flowers of the smoke bush are delicate, so they need a lightweight leaf material. The new material I've found is sold by several suppliers. The one I like best is made by Noch and imported from Germany. The leaf material comes in several colors, and a little goes a long way.

Spray the smoke bush tree with flat acrylic varnish and sprinkle on the leaves. I like to use several

shades of green on the same tree. The varnish dries in about 20 minutes; if the leaf cover looks sparse, just spray again.

STRENGTHENING SMOKE-BUSH TREES

A friend was experimenting with building smoke bush trees and found a neat way to strengthen the fragile dried flowers. He dipped them in Minwax Wood Hardener (this stuff is made to harden rotted wood) and let them dry. Wood Hardener penetrates the cells and leaves behind a shellac or resin that gives them strength. It can be found in paint and hardware stores.

BUMPY CHENILLE TREES IN THE BACKGROUND

Bumpy chenille is truly a new wrinkle on an old trick. Here's how to use this common craft material to make background pine trees in larger scales and

good-looking foreground pine trees in N scale.

First, look through your local craft store for green bumpy chenille. It's easy to recognize because individual strands look like large irregular pipe cleaners, each about a foot long. Buy a couple of packages of dark green and brown to experiment with.

Cut each bumpy chenille strand with wire cutters into six or eight pieces, varying the height of each tree. They can be glued in place as is, but they're too shiny to look like real pines. I glue the trees to cardboard with Walther's Goo. After the glue dries I take the cardboard outdoors and paint the trees dark green with a spray can. While the paint is wet I sprinkle on fine forest green scenic foam, with a few other shades of pine-green or blue-green foam for variety.

After the paint dries, remove the trees from the cardboard and glue them between your background deciduous trees.

BUMPY CHENILLE TREES IN THE FOREGROUND

Bumpy chenille can be used in the foreground. On HO and larger layouts I've landscaped around structures with bumpy chenille tips, using them as trimmed ornamental pines and with other trees in clusters. The only difference in making foreground and background trees is that more texture is added to the foreground trees.

Cut the bumpy chenille into tree-shaped cones and put a dab of white glue on each end to keep the fibers from falling out. After the glue dries, cement each tree to a 2" square of cardboard.

Spray each tree with diluted white glue, matte medium, or spray adhesive. Turn each tree upside down and sprinkle on dark green foam, then shake off the excess over a sheet of newspaper. Turn the tree right side up and sprinkle medium-green or blue-green foam on the upper surfaces. After the glue dries, remove the tree from the cardboard square before adding it to your scenery.

BIRCH TREES FOR VARIETY AND CONTRAST

For scenic variety — and to add color to the forest — I install birch trees. Real birch trees come in many different bark colors; from reddish-brown to white,

but I build only white birches because they're so easily recognized. Paint the trunk white, then add the characteristic black scars. You can paint the scars, but an easy, no-mess alternative is to draw them with a black marking pen.

LOOFAH SPONGE PINE TREES

Natural loofah sponges, popular with the ladies for removing dry skin, can often be found on sale in

drugstores. The interior of the sponge makes good-looking foliage for pine trees. Using a long, thin-bladed knife, remove the conical core.

Before slicing the core balogna-style into thin

wafers, color it. Put several teaspoons of dark green Rit or Tintex fabric dye into a saucepan of boiling water. Add the sponge pieces and stir until they absorb the dye and change color. Place on newspaper and let dry overnight.

Slice the colored loofah into wafers and slide them onto a tapered tree trunk. Start with large wafers, placing them closest to the ground. Keep impaling smaller ones (leave about 1/4" between wafers), finishing with the smallest at the top. Add a drop of white glue where the trunk and each wafer meet. When the glue dries, spray the tree with diluted white glue and sprinkle on fine forest-green foam.

HANDY LICHEN STICKS

I've got an assortment of log-like lichen sticks made from 1"-square Styrofoam bars. One of my favorite uses for them is camouflaging the back edge of an open-top holding yard, making it look as though closer texture continues in the background.

Making the sticks is simple: Cut 1"-thick Styrofoam into 1" strips, paint them a dark green or dark earth color, add some cheap texture like sawdust, cork-roadbed sandings, or badly colored foam,

and glue lichen clumps to the top surface with white or yellow glue. I use RC modelers' T-pins to hold the lichen in place until the glue dries. The sticks also come in handy as props when shooting photos elsewhere out on the layout.

TOOTHPICK PINE TREES

Dick Patterson's layout has thousands of the best western-style miniature pine trees I've seen. They're made from toothpick trunks with sawdust for the shape and texture. Here's his recipe:

First, empty a box of common flat toothpicks into a jar of brown or black stain. After they have absorbed the stain, remove them and spread on paper towels to dry.

Decide on the best heights for the trees and cut the toothpicks with a pair of wire cutters. I cut some in half and leave some whole. Next, pick up a toothpick and dip the top half in full-strength white glue, then plunge it into dark green sawdust or coarse forest green scenic foam. Lay the toothpick on a sheet of plastic wrap or waxed paper to dry. It's okay that one

side of the toothpick will be flat—just place that side toward the background.

Dick uses several sizes of these trees on his

layout, from the tallest, about 2" high, to the smallest, about ½" high against the backdrop. (The large photo on page 16 shows the finished effect.) He mounts his trees on the scenery with drops of clear hot glue. He drizzles the hot glue on the scenery and sets the trees upright into the puddle. You can place these small trees as fast as you can move using this method. After the glue cools, the trees are held upright and the glue disappears.

REMOVABLE TREES EVERYWHERE!

Dick Patterson has a beautiful layout based upon the Dolly Varden Mine that was located on Prince Rupert Sound in British Columbia. The layout features hundreds of pine trees made made from dried Pride of Madeira weed branches glued onto carved balsa trunks. All Dick's trees are mounted on pins protruding up from the scenery.

Dick fixes the pins in place by first making ¼" circles from shirt cardboard using a paper punch. He inserts a small dressmaker's pin in the center of each circle, then glues the circles, with the pins sticking upward, to his scenery with drops of white glue.

After painting and scenicking, the punched-cardboard bases become invisible, and Dick just pushes the balsa trunks down onto the pins. Individual trees can be moved, removed, or repaired without drilling new holes in the scenery or filling old ones.

But beware! Don't do what I did and lean on the treeless scenery — if you do, you'll learn painfully about the "porcupine effect"!

PLANTING A STRUCTURE IN THE TREES

Sometimes you want to create the illusion that there's more to the village than just the few foreground structures that your visitors can see. I like to have several buildings trail off into the woods at the end of the street, or disappear behind rocks, telephone poles, and fences.

It's easy to suggest that there's something in the woods behind the main street. All you need is the tops of several trees and a piece of a structure. One side, a roof, and a chimney is usually enough, as the photo I shot on Tom Wilson's layout shows.

Set the building behind and away from the main structures, or cut it on an angle and glue it to the backdrop. Then add the treetops. I glue these directly to the structure, to the surrounding trees, and to each other. I like to hide the building so just the roof, a little wall, and the chimney shows. The more foliage you glue around the structure the better it will look. As you may have guessed, smaller scale structures look even better, helping to force the perspective of the scene. Also, structures at eye level, like those on the top of a hill, will look most realistic.

The layout here is HO scale, but the Bachmann farmhouse is N scale — yet the overall scene works! Note the HO figure positioned beside the farmhouse to give away the illusion.

3
Forced perspective and backdrops

Making the most of your space

WHETHER YOUR LAYOUT is 4' x 8' or 40' x 80', you still don't have enough space to create a complete miniature world. (Even if you had the space, you wouldn't have the time!) So the name of the game becomes trickery: modeling the right things to tell your story, and modeling just enough of them in such a way that what isn't there is implied.

Generally speaking, foreground areas are devoted to tracks, trains, and the stations and industries they serve, so most of our trickery comes into play in the region on the other side of the tracks, away from the viewer. The first (and probably the best) ruse is to add a sky backdrop. No other improvement will make such an immediate positive

change in viewing your layout. Next comes painting scenery on the blue sky, maybe even detailed background scenes, if you've got the talent. Yet another approach is adding background models in scales smaller than your trains.

Here's a short chapter filled with ways to make your limited real estate seem a whole lot bigger than it really is.

USING FORCED PERSPECTIVE

A lot has been written on forced perspective, the idea of using full-scale models in the foreground and progressively smaller models behind them to enhance the illusion of depth. I even recall someone trying to work it all out mathematically.

The fact is that it's a whole lot easier than that. Forced perspective works every time! And it's not just for the camera; your eye and mind will automatically take in a forced-perspective scene and see it not as buildings in two different scales, but as a convincing scene. You can go so far as to butt HO buildings on the close side of the track and N scale buildings on the far side, and it looks just fine.

This idea is simple, and it holds great promise. I'm waiting or the first fellow who does a whole layout this way — it should be fabulous.

N SCALE BUILDINGS FOR FORCED PERSPECTIVE

If your trains are HO scale, N scale presents the perfect source of forced-perspective models. Building N scale plastic kits is just as easy as building regular HO models, and the main challenge is to paint them down a bit more than you would foreground models. Add white and gray to the colors you would usually use.

At least one manufacturer, Bachmann, offers built-up N scale buildings. These can be touch-up painted and used as is, or carefully disassembled and spruced up before reassembly. Focus your improvements on the roof — which is often sub-par — and the paint job, where washes and dry-brushing can bring even a fairly crude model up to snuff.

N SCALE PRINTED BACKDROPS FOR AN HO LAYOUT

Many layouts use the same commercial printed backdrops, and even the best-executed foreground can be lost when the background is a cliché and pulls

the eye away from the foreground. One way to get around the sameness of printed backdrops is to mix several scales in the same scene. I glue pieces of N scale backgrounds both in front of and behind the cut-out HO background sections, and swap around the signs on some of the buildings. This breaks up familiar scenes and structures into less-recogniz-

able individual shapes and overall compositions.

To mount the cut-out sections, brush thinned white glue on the backdrop and on both sides of the paper. Slide the sections into place, adjust the positions, and brush another coat of glue over the surface. The glue will flatten and smooth the cut-outs, but while it dries they may buckle and bubble. Leave them alone; the wrinkles usually disappear when the glue dries.

These mixed-scale backdrops are especially good for eye-level areas and behind a lot of structures.

USING PRINTED BACKGROUND FLATS

Walthers makes several sets of printed background building flats called Instant Buildings. They can quickly provide a busy and purposeful-looking background for a town or city scene, and even if you plan to eventually replace them with 3-D low-relief walls from structure kits, they can bring a complex scene to life quickly. (Confession: The temporary flats in the photo have been in place for more than five years.)

Instead of gluing the sheets to your backdrop, carefully cut them out with scissors and a sharp modeling knife, then mount the pieces to ⅛" Upson

Board or Fome-cor. Trim the edges of the backing, then paint with flat black Polly S.

I add a piece of $^3/_4$"-square wood along the bottom edge of each flat to stiffen it, then glue a couple of scrap lead weights to the top edge of the stiffener to make the flat less likely to tip over. Leaving the flats loose means you can reposition them to check the visual effect of various arrangements, and this will help when it comes time to replace them with 3-D versions — if you ever get around to it!

BACKDROP HEIGHT

For maximum realism the height of your backdrop is important. Ideally, it should reach from the top of your benchwork to the ceiling. The horizon line should be at about average eye level (about 66" from your floor), and tall background features, including mountains, big buildings, and smokestacks, should be above your viewers' eye level.

But this isn't always possible. When you can't achieve the optimum height, come as close as you can. This could mean working on your layout at a moderately uncomfortable high level (that's what step stools are for), or taking the approach that well-known modeler John Olson did with his HOn3 Mescal Lines a few years back. John originally built the benchwork at a convenient working height — about 46" — but planned all along to raise the whole railroad another foot or so to a better level for viewing.

CHOOSING AND APPLYING BACKDROP PAINTS

A backdrop doesn't have to be a work of art to be effective, and even an unadorned blue sky will add a lot of distance behind your benchwork. Whichever route you choose to travel, the first step is to erect a seamless backdrop surface and roll on a couple of coats of blue sky color. (Don't ever let anybody sell you on a gray or mostly cloudy sky. Indoor model railroading ought be an all-good-weather hobby!)

A close match is Montgomery Ward Tahoe Blue (187-B-3-71). If there isn't a Montgomery Ward store near you, most large paint stores with a computerized mixing machine can look up the number and mix a close duplicate.

Before you start painting mix all your paint. Mix enough to do the whole backdrop, even if you're only planning to paint a small section. Because it's tough to precisely match the sky color, plan on having at least a full quart of your basic blue left over for future touch-ups, and put together a master color chip chart with all formulas so you can match them later if need be.

NO BLUE CEILINGS, PLEASE!

The sky is blue, so in addition to painting your

vertical backdrop blue, you ought to continue the blue up onto the ceiling, right?

Wrong! Even if you've gone to the trouble to cove your backdrop up into the ceiling, paint the transition blue, but then switch to bright flat white ceiling paint. There are two reasons for this: You want the ceiling to reflect as much light as possible back onto the railroad, maximizing the effectiveness of your lighting. Most model railroads are too dark to begin with, and a blue ceiling absorbs more light than it reflects. And when it comes time to photograph your layout, a blue ceiling will add so much blue even to strong photo lighting that the color balance of the film will be thrown off.

LIGHTING FIRST

Installing lighting before starting on scenery is always good practice, but having your final lighting in place is especially important before the background is painted. All shadows painted on the back-

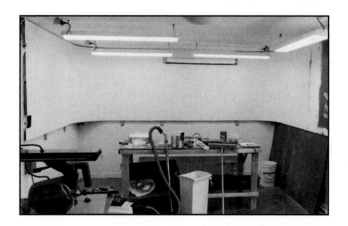

ground should fall in the same direction as those in the foreground that are caused by the room lights. The lights you choose will effect the way the backdrop colors look, and better yet, good lighting will help you see what you're doing as you build both foreground and background areas.

TWO-LAYER BACKDROPS

Some modelers have experimented with two-layer backdrops. The rear layer is the usual blue sky backdrop that's behind the layout and extends around the walls. In front of this is a closer backdrop made from Styrofoam or screen wire which has been cut into mountain profiles. These foreground flats are covered with small bits of lichen and different shades of scenic foam. When used effectively they give the background scenery a three-dimensional quality that's hard to achieve in other ways.

HELP FOR PAINTING BACKDROPS

I've never had much ambition to be a two-dimensional landscape painter, so any shortcut to achieving a convincing backdrop sounds good to me. Here's one approach, with little or no talent required!

Choose a suitable background from color slides taken in the area you're modeling. Turn off the room lights and project the slides directly onto the backdrop. Choose the slide that's best for the first background section, and try angling the projector to find the best match of the slide with your foreground scenery.

Trace the projected outlines of hills or mountains with a No. 2 lead pencil. Project the next slide, mating it to the first so the contours line up. Again trace the outline, repeating the process until all the background has been traced. (To use the same slides over and over, stretch the scene by placing the projector at an extreme angle to the background. Slides can also be reversed in the projector.)

Now turn on the room lights and touch up any lines that don't quite meet. Start painting with the most distant hills, then work forward. Be sure to mix enough of each color to paint all of the background, and store leftover paint in clearly labeled jars. Dave's

book, *How to Build Realistic Model Railroad Scenery*, has detailed recipes for background colors.

FIXING CRACKS IN THE BACKDROP

For years I've used either linoleum runner or ⅛" Masonite screwed to a frame as the seamless backdrops around my model railroads. I covered the seams where the pieces of backdrop joined with drywall tape and coated the tape with joint compound. The joints were sanded smooth and primed — along with the rest of the backdrop — with flat white paint.

This method makes an almost invisible seam for a while, but after several seasons of expansion and contraction from changing heat and humidity the seams may crack and open slightly. The cracks are hard to repair: Filling and sanding the crack is easy, but matching the paint is next to impossible.

When visiting a large model railroad with a long run of seamless backdrop I was impressed that there were no cracks — even though the layout was over 10 years old. I asked the owner and he explained his solution. He uses wallpaper paste to glue long strips of linoleum underlayment paper over the traditional Masonite backdrop. The underlayment is a thick, matte-surface paper that will stretch and shrink with seasonal changes. It can be primed and painted just like other popular background materials. Underlayment paper is available at most floor-covering dealers.

PLASTIC BACKDROP MATERIAL

One of the best materials I've found for building backdrops, for making structure bases, and for modeling pavement is called Komatex. It was recommended by a plastics distributor who I found in the Yellow Pages. He said Komatex is used to make outdoor signs.

Komatex is a PVC (polyvinyl chloride) product that is sold in 4' x 8' sheets, in 13 different colors, and in thicknesses from 1 to 13mm. It's also inexpensive: My first 4' x 8' by 1mm-thick sheet cost only $16. It looks and works like styrene, can be cut with a mat knife, and responds to MEK (methyl-ethyl-ketone) solvent. One side is glassy smooth and the other has an eggshell finish. It can be shaped with heat and welded using a hot-air PVC welding tool.

To make the backdrop I mounted the 4' x 8' sheet on a wood frame, glossy side out, using Liquid Nails construction adhesive and staples. I sprayed the surface with flat blue, starting at the top and working toward the center, and flat white paint, working from the bottom up. I used cheap spray colors; one can of each color was enough for a 4' x 8' sheet.

COLORS FOR THE FRONT BOARD OF YOUR LAYOUT

A model railroad is a total presentation, and how you treat the front edge of your layout is an important factor. I've tried simply rolling the scenery over the front edge and ignoring the problem of mounting controls and such. While this works well for photography, it's less than satisfactory for operating and viewing the layout in person.

What seems to work best is a plain Masonite surface painted with semigloss paint. Gloss paint is too shiny, and a flat color quickly shows fingerprints and even minor scratches. With that established, you have to choose a color.

My favorite is deep medium-dark green (I use Valspar-brand No. 22-10 Crater). From a distance this color blends into the overall green of my State of Maine scenery, becoming invisible. (The front board color shouldn't draw attention to itself. That's why fancy textures like wood grain don't work for me. Flat black, which sounds like a good idea, doesn't work either — it's too dead.)

Jim Kelly built a Southern Pacific Tehachapi Pass layout a few years back and painted the front board a rich reddish-brown, just a bit more on the brown side than maroon. The color nicely complemented Jim's desert scenery without calling attention to itself, and the red was far more pleasing than the chocolate brown I've seen on a few layouts. Like black, dark brown is just too overpowering, especially if your layout has relatively deep front boards to accommodate control panels, switching maps, and so forth.

A TEMPORARY BACKDROP

I needed a quick background to surround a project I was building. The quickest and most economical solution was using 1/8" tempered Masonite mounted on a frame of 1 x 2 strapping. I attached everything to the walls with removable drywall screws. The tempered Masonite will make gentle curves in the corners without support or cracking.

I taped and spackled the joints between the Masonite sections, then sanded, primed, and covered with two finish coats of sky blue. After the project was completed and photographed I took the temporary backdrop apart and returned the room to normal.

QUICK CLOUDS ON YOUR BACKDROP

A solid blue backdrop is better than no backdrop, but it can be pretty boring. I like to add a little spice and variety with clouds. These clouds are so simple that anyone can paint them!

Start with flat white spray paint, the kind sold in hardware stores. Lightly spray on straight lines of varying lengths holding the spray can at least 24" from the backdrop. These streaks should look light

and fleecy, like thin high cirrus clouds.

Next add several big cumulus clouds. These have flat bottoms and large, puffy tops. Spray in a circular motion, and be sure to use several light applications to avoid sags. You can get fancy by adding a light gray shadow to the bottoms of your cumulus clouds. Just spray a light, straight, gray line on the undersides.

While you're spraying clouds, take a moment, step back, and evaluate them. How do they look? Do you need to vary the cloud sizes from area to area?

Are they too big and too puffy? If they don't look right, walk away and come back hours, even days, later. If the clouds still don't please you, grab a wide brush and repaint the background with sky blue and start again. Practice will help.

Spray paint generates a lot of overspray. Be sure to cover the layout with an old sheet, wear a respirator, and provide plenty of ventilation.

It's low tide — permanently — on the waterfront at Cundy's Harbor on Bob's Carrabasset & Dead River. The distinctive lines, patterns, and colors of the sea provide a dramatic contrast to the more familiar railroad action.

4
On the waterfront

Modeling where the trains come down to meet the ships

THERE'S SOMETHING SPECIAL about waterfront modeling. Both authors of this book grew up in the same New England seacoast town near Boston, Massachusetts, and both of us have built layouts that incorporate waterfront scenes. The combination of railroading with waterfront industries such as canneries and boatyards is a winner. Strong vertical elements provided by ships, boats, and weatherbeaten pilings provide a superb counterpoint to the predominantly horizontal lines of trains and track. Here's a handful of ideas to help bring your coast, lakefront, or riverside scenes to life.

WATERFRONT REFERENCE PHOTOS

I've always been fascinated by waterfront architecture. I've spent many weekends, armed with my pocket automatic camera, capturing the unique look of these structures. I shoot color prints because they're easier to handle and view than color slides.

Storing, then finding, the photos was a problem until I found clear plastic print storage pages in the photo store. Each two-sided page holds three prints a side. The pages fit in standard three-ring binders which will lie flat on the workbench.

When it's time to build a model of one of these

modeling enamels. The epoxy formulation probably won't react with the enamels, but always mix a small test batch, both to check the compatibility and to assess the coloring effect of the paint.

MARKING THE TIDE LINE

Every seaside waterfront has a discernible tide line, the height that the average high tide rises to every six hours or so. The height of the line above low water varies with latitude (the farther north you get from the equator, the greater the height). Folks in Florida only have a one- or two-foot tide fall, while visitors to Maine will notice that it's as much as 14 feet. It's wise to collect color photos of the waterfront of the area you're modeling to see tide height, types and colors of seaweed, and colors of the surrounding rocks.

structures, or just check a few of the details, I remove the pages I need from the album and bring them to my workbench. Because the plastic is stiff I can lean the pages against the wall for ready reference.

SIMULATING WATER WITH ENVIROTEX

Envirotex epoxy decoupage resin has been a favorite for modeling water for almost 20 years. It's easy to mix, almost odorless, and the epoxy formula-

tion won't damage Styrofoam scenery. Here are a couple of tricks for using it.

Always mix a small batch of Envirotex in a paper cup the night before you pour the water to make sure it's going to solidify. The possibility of pouring the stuff and having it not cure is just too awful to even think about.

If you're willing to spend the extra time, you can prod the Envirotex while it sets and get some nice ripples in the finished water. Use any fairly blunt tool to work ripples into your Envirotex as it sets — my favorite is a new, clean Popsicle or craft stick.

To tint Envirotex try adding small amounts of flat

Most modelers, especially in the smaller scales, will want to build their waterfronts as they look at low water. This means they can exaggerate the height of the tide line more than what's prototypically correct. A higher-than-normal tide line looks better.

The tide line should be a constant height around the waterfront. To mark the line, tape a scribe or a pencil to a block of wood at the right height. Slide the scriber on the flat surface where the water will be. Push the point of the scriber or pencil against the scenery just hard enough to make a mark.

. . . AND PAINTING IT

I model New England, so I paint everything below the tide line a darker shade of the color above the line. This color is made by adding a few drops each of brown and black to the base color. After the paint dries, brush diluted white glue (1 part glue to 1 part water) into the tide area. While it's wet push small pieces of sphagnum moss, coarse brown scenic foam, and strands of fake hair material (like Timber Products Wild Weeds) into the glue to represent clumps of seaweed. Only the texture is important since all the seaweed will be painted.

The color of seaweed can vary from yellow to light green, brownish-green, dark brown, or a combination of these colors. In New England rockweed is the most common seaweed and it's a reddish-brown color. Below the waterline is one of the few places in model railroading where it's okay to use gloss paints.

. . . AND COLORING THE SEAWEED

Use acrylics, straight from the tube, to paint seaweed. Streak the paint on, mixing the colors on the seaweed itself. After the colors dry, give them a coat of gloss medium to increase the wet look. Everything below the tide line stays wet even at low tide.

I've written before about making barnacles, so we need just a quick review here. Fill a paper cup with

a little less diluted white glue than the height of the tide line. Dip pilings in the glue, drain, then sprinkle fine white ballast over the glue. Scrape away any ballast clinging to the bottom of the pilings. Barnacles usually grow thickest on man-made objects such as piers, pilings, bridge abutments, and retaining walls.

LESS-REGULAR PILINGS

Pilings are an important detail along the waterfront, and you can't have too many of them. The traditional way to make pilings is to heavily distress common birch dowels to add a rough wood grain texture, then cut to length and install.

But dowels are too regular. In any given scale you'll only be able to use two of the standard sizes, and there's no taper as there often is on the real thing. You can make dowel pilings a bit more gnarly looking by roughing them up with a coarse sanding

drum in a motor tool before distressing. Take one or two and break them with a twisting motion to represent pilings broken off during a rough landing by one of the local captains.

I also make pilings from the handles of worn-out

artist's brushes. Remove the paint or varnish with furniture stripper, add texture by drawing a razor saw blade along the length of the handle, follow up with a file card, then a suede brush, then paint or stain the piling stock and cut the pieces you need. The subtle taper of various sections of the handles will add a realistic irregular look to the overall scene, even if most of your pilings do have to be made from dowels.

LESS ROOF OVERHANG ON WATERFRONT BUILDINGS

Most kit structures, including those intended for waterfront use, come with substantial roof overhang. There are undoubtedly prototype buildings that prove this is correct, but one characteristic feature of seashore buildings is little, if any, roof overhang. Many East Coast pierside sheds have none at all.

When you build kit structures for your water-

front, try trimming back the edges of the roof parts. This trick works well for structures elsewhere, but it's an essential part of seacoast flavor.

DRIPS AND SPILLS

Paint a trail of full-strength acrylic gloss medium across your pier or wharf to represent a leaky bucket or tank. The gloss medium will catch the light and

make your viewer wonder — just for a moment — if that spot is really wet.

FINDING HULLS FOR BOATS AND SHIPS

Building ships and boats for your waterfront is fairly easy once you have a workable hull shape. While the traditional ways to make wood hulls are enjoyable, they're time-consuming. I keep them in reserve as a last resort for modeling that special boat that I simply have to have to make the scene.

A better way is to look for hulls in inexpensive plastic boat and ship kits, even toys. This is easier than you think, because hulls don't have any real scale: If the shape is right, a hull can be a large one

in N scale or a small one in HO or O. Superstructure parts have to be people-size, and therefore carefully scaled, but with hulls what you want is a good shape that's about the right size for the boat you're setting out to model. One of my HO scale lobster boats, for instance, started life as a whaleboat from Revell's big USS *Constitution*.

For HO or N scale a good start on several projects is a kit from Lindberg called the "Waterfront Four" (No. 72120), which provides four boats that appear to be roughly N scale. The hulls are great for HO, though, and with a few scratchbuilt cabin parts (or better yet, parts taken from another kit that's close to HO), they'll have you well on your way toward different and distinctive small craft for your waterfront.

REPLACEMENT MASTS AND SPARS

Styrene ship kits are my favorite source for making ship and boat models, but occasionally I'll run up against a situation where the plastic masts or spars aren't stiff enough to carry taut rigging lines.

The solution is to replace the plastic parts with spars whittled from birch dowel. Compared to the molded styrene parts the birch is extremely strong — strong enough to stand tall and straight under the tension applied by rigging.

ADJUSTABLE RIGGING

Ships and boats have two kinds of wire or rope rigging: standing and running. Standing rigging consists of stays, guy wires, and other fixed lines that hold masts and other parts of the ship in place; running rigging is adjusted to sail the ship, do its work, or handle cargo. While all these ropes don't have to be 100 percent accurate for model railroad purposes, they should at least look purposeful, and this trick with standing rigging can help make your boat models stand straight and tall.

I rig mast stays so the lines pass through Northeastern brand miniature eyepins inside the bulwarks (walls) of the boat and at the tops of the masts.

I tie the stay to one eyebolt on the port side, and run it up to the masthead. Then, instead of tying the stay off there I cross it over the mast, run it down to one of the starboard staybolts, through the second one, back up the mast again, and back down on the port side.

After pulling light tension on the line, I tie it off on the other staybolts on the port side, but leave the line free to slip at the top of the mast. With this arrangement I can push the mast left or right to straighten it, and the stays will still remain taut on both sides.

SOURCES FOR NAUTICAL DETAILS

Ship modeling is an even older hobby than model railroading, and the fittings you'll need to detail ships and boats and establish character along your waterfront are available as ship model parts. Scale isn't as important for these parts as it is for train

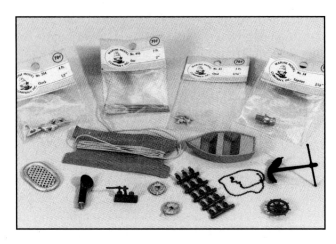

fittings, and the thing to do is ignore the package labels and browse through the packages looking for items that will look close enough for your scale.

If you're really into waterfront modeling, look for surplus or half-built plastic ship kits at swap meets or yard sales (a lot more of those three-foot-long Revell *Constitutions* and *Cutty Sarks* are started than finished, and they're a treasure-trove of boats, rigging, ship's wheels, anchors, and dozens of other useful parts).

ALL HANDS — AND DETAIL — ON DECK!

It's important to remember that most boats are working businesses, and should have clutter on deck and crew members on the scene. For a fishing vessel this means nets, bait boxes, and evidence of the catch; for a tugboat you'll need towing cables, mooring lines, and seamen to handle them. Add a couple of barrels, a few neatly coiled ropes, a first mate, and maybe a ship's dog, and your beautifully made boat will be more than a well-executed model — it will come to life.

A PAIR OF CONVINCING HO EAST-COAST FISHING BOATS

A couple of years back I kitbashed two 1940s-era Maine sardine carriers loosely based on designs I found in *Boat Modeling the Easy Way*, by Harold "Dynamite" Payson (International Marine, Camden, Maine, 1994). They turned out better than I expected, so here are photos and a few construction details here should you want to do the same.

The first conversion, christened *West Sider*, was based on the hull of the old 1/96 scale Revell harbor tug. I used the hull virtually unmodified, but cut

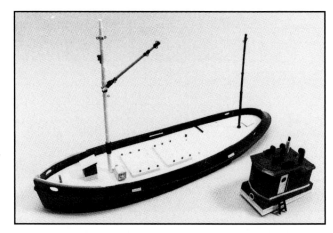

down the tug superstructure to make the simple one-deck pilot house on the fishing craft.

Masts, ventilators, and several other details came from the tugboat kit and my collection of ship kit parts, and I made the hatches from Evergreen styrene sheet and strip.

The second model, *Virginia*, has the same general lines, but its slightly longer hull was made by chopping and lengthening the hull from a Heller 1/60 scale *Kurun* sailboat (kit No. 80614). I built the pilot

house from styrene sheet, the mast and boom came from the *Kurun* kit, and the rest of the details were derived just like those on the Revell-based boat.

Both models have just enough rigging to make them convincing, plus plenty of topside details to make them look like honest-to-goodness workaday fishing vessels.

A SLIGHT — BUT REALISTIC — LIST

Boats and ships are constantly in motion, even when they're tied up to a pier or dock. The slightest breeze or sea swell will start even a small boat swaying gently, and you can model this effect on your scale waterfront.

When you cut a boat hull down to the waterline, sand it flat by rubbing the rough-cut hull against a sheet of wet-or-dry sandpaper glued to a sheet of glass. Keep the fore-and-aft trim as level as you can, but allow a few degrees of port or starboard list to creep in. When this particular boat is added to your waterfront, the effect will be that all the boats are gently rocking from side to side — even the ones that are perfectly upright!

The only caution is to make most of your boats vertical: If they're all swaying, the effect will be that you simply can't get any of them to stand straight!

PHOTOETCHED LOBSTER TRAPS

Builders in Scale (see Addresses) offers a nice set of four lacy photoetched lobster traps for HO scale. They're pricey, like a lot of photoetched stuff, but a few of them are just the thing to accent the extreme foreground of your waterfront scene. They're a bit large, so while they look fine in HO, you can probably get away with using them in S scale, even O.

DUST ON THE WATERFRONT

Dust is a problem everywhere on every model railroad, but a dark, shiny water surface really makes it show up ugly. Nothing looks less realistic than dust and lint particles seemingly floating on top of what's supposed to be a wet surface.

The first line of defense against such dust is eliminating it at the source, and this means a tight ceiling over your railroad, a sealed or carpeted floor, and a prohibition on doing dusty jobs like sanding or spray painting in the layout area. Most of us can't afford to build a layout in a high-tech clean room, though, so we have to talk about cleaning the water.

Regardless of what you've used for your water surface you'll want a gentle means of dusting it. I keep an inexpensive feather duster (yes, they still make them!) on hand which I use only on water, and I have a soft-bristled dusting brush dedicated to the same task. I start with the feather duster for broad areas, then use the soft brush to sweep around piers and pilings.

But the most important tip is to design your waterfront so it can be cleaned. I've made the decks of several piers removable, so I can lift them off to dust the water below them. (This feature will also make it easier to renew the water surface a few years down the road, which I know I'll eventually have to do.) Most important of all, the

lift-off decks also mean I won't have huge dust bunnies lurking beneath the wharf to spoil my carefully built illusion of wet water.

DUST ON THE WATERFRONT II

When you break out the vacuum to clean your waterfront, take it easy around the water itself. Everything we use for modeling water scratches easily, and dinging the surface with the shop-vac nozzle is all too easy.

I bought a kit of special mini-attachments for my vacuum cleaner; it has small-diameter nozzles and

a couple of soft-bristled brush fittings, along with an adapter and flexible plastic hose to mate them to a standard vacuum cleaner. My fittings kit came from Walthers (No. 312-1, $16.95), but I've seen the same item in computer catalogs and office-supply stores, where they're offered for sucking dust out of office machines and keyboards.

A SOURCE OF HO BOATS

J.D. Innovations (see Addresses) has introduced several HO scale cast resin boat kits in the past couple of years. If you want to populate your waterfront quickly, these offer a good way to do it. The kits are fairly basic, but the shapes are attractive and the resin takes paint and glues well.

Figures are mighty important players in telling the stories on your railroad. Use wax, not glue, to hold them in place.

5
Tricks with figures and vehicles

Adding supporting actors to your scenes — on foot and on the road

TRAINS ARE THE LEADING MEN and leading ladies in the dramatic life of a model railroad, but they need supporting actors. Figures are obvious choices to play this role, and so are vehicles. In fact, nothing works quite as well as cars and trucks to establish the era of your layout. Your visitors may not know anything at all about the prototype railroad you're modeling, but a lot of them will be able to spot a '57 Chevy or '40 Ford a mile away. If you model early railroading, the presence of horse-drawn wagons and the absence of motor vehicles will put your era across quickly and succinctly.

But it's possible to have too much of a good thing! Too many figures can make a scene crowded when the effect you want is only busy. And even though I enjoy building vehicles — it's almost a hobby within a hobby for me — it's important to use them with dramatic pacing. Most cars and trucks should be parked, just as in real life, and those that are supposedly moving on the road should be spaced out at considerable distances. (Even in HO or N scale tailgating just doesn't look good, nor does a traffic jam!)

MORTICIAN'S AND DOLLHOUSE WAX FOR PLACING FIGURES

Ever heard of "Mortician's Wax"? Well, you don't have to be a mortician to buy it (check a theatrical costume shop, or ask a dollhouse miniatures shop for "tacky wax"), and it makes an excellent temporary stickum for fastening figures in place. That "temporary" is important, because you should never place figures permanently on your layout. Leaving them movable means you can revise the story a scene tells just by swapping the players.

The wax is tacky enough to hold the figures in place with just a dab on each foot, but it won't pull the paint off the shoes, and it won't remove foam or other texture from your layout as white glue will. You can remove what little residue the wax leaves with a rag moistened with cigarette lighter fluid (benzine).

Once you've got a cake of this wax in your bag of tricks you'll find it's great for setting up hard-to-hold detail parts for airbrushing, and you can even use it to hold parts in place temporarily to paint or weather them before final assembly.

HANDLES FOR PAINTING FIGURES

You can't possibly paint figures well unless you can hold them comfortably. Make up a couple of 6" lengths of 1¼" dowel, flat at both ends, so you can get a handle on the job.

Attach the figures by the feet to the stands with white or yellow glue (heavy O scale metal figures may require a reinforcing pin in one of the legs that you can insert in the dowel). Wrap the fingers of your non-brush hand around the dowel while painting,

and rest your forearm and elbow on the bench to steady them. Then, when you're done, pry the figure loose with a single-edge razor blade and touch up the feet if necessary.

ROLLING — ER, THAT'S PAINTING — YOUR OWN

Even a small layout, diorama, or module can easily soak up dozens of figures, but at more than a dollar apiece, assembling a crowd of ready-painted figures quickly becomes pricey.

One solution is to buy unpainted plastic figures in

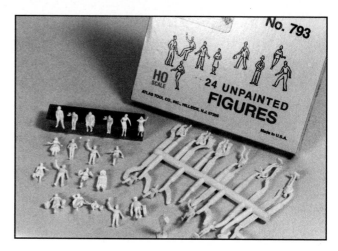

bulk. Atlas has one set in HO (No. 763), and Preiser offers over a dozen in HO, several of them containing 120 excellent figures (see the Walthers catalog). The price noodles out to less than 25 cents per figure, so if you're willing to spend the time and pitch in a few dabs of paint, you can populate your scene for a good deal less than paying for the high-priced help!

YOU CAN PAINT IT!

It may seem pretty obvious, but one of the great truths of painting figures or any other detail item was revealed to me several years ago by a military figure painter. His guidance was simple: "If you can see it, you can paint it."

Those are words to live by, and they're true. It may not be easy, and you may need a tiny brush or a drop of paint on the end of a fine wire and 13 tries, but if you can see a detail, however small, you can somehow get a dab of color on it. Just knowing this has always been a great confidence builder for me!

And if you *can't* see it, by golly, you don't need to paint it!

PAINTING HO AND SMALLER FIGURES

While the fussy techniques that military figure-painting hobbyists use will work for O scale and even S, they're too time-consuming for HO. Here's a modified, six-step version I use for HO and N:

1. Prepare the figures. Go over each figure, whether metal or plastic, to remove flash and mold-

where shirt meets pants, hat intersects head, and so on. You'll be surprised at how much this simple technique brings out the molded-in detail. If the wash obscures broad areas of the figure, remove it with a brush moistened in mineral spirits.

5. Dry-brush the highlights and details. Let the brown wash dry overnight or more (oil color takes a long time to dry). Then lightly dry-brush the figure's clothing with off white, keeping the color off flesh areas. It's better to err on the side of too little dry-brushing; the wash does most of the work.

6. Finish with flat. Complete the job a with an airbrushed coat of Testor Dullcote, then head for your layout or diorama to add that much-needed touch of life to your scene.

ing lines. A fine suede brush works well on metal figures to polish up the surface and whisk away thin parting lines; otherwise use a No. 11 X-acto blade and needle files.

2. Prime. Airbrush at least a dozen figures at a time with a basic flesh color like Floquil Foundation or Flesh. Let this dry a week — better yet, forget about the figures and let them dry for a couple of weeks.

3. Color clothes and details. Paint clothing, shoes, and details with acrylic model paints. Use Tamiya or Polly S flat paints. Make these base (or undercoat) colors fairly bright; remember, the figures on your layout should provide accent colors and help to direct attention around your scenes. Now let the base colors dry. These paints dry fast, and a couple of hours or overnight is usually enough.

4. Deepen shadows with a wash. Make up a thin wash consisting of a 1/2" squiggle of burnt umber oil color in one cup of mineral spirits (paint thinner). Flow this onto the figures with a wide brush, or dip the figures into the wash, then stand them up to let dry. Repeat if necessary. The idea of the wash is to let the brown flow into shadow areas and form boundary lines between colors at natural breaks —

IMPROVING COMMERCIAL PAINTED FIGURES

They're often expensive, but ready-to-go painted figures are an excellent way to populate your layout in a hurry. Good as they are, they can benefit from a bit of extra attention before they become citizens of your lineside towns.

Start by examining each figure for bad casting

lines or obvious painting mistakes. Correct these with a few swipes from a knife or file, then touch up the paint. Follow steps three through six of the regular figure-painting sequence (above), then sign up your figures as brand-new taxpayers — and new patrons for your passenger trains!

MODELING A CROWD

You won't run up against this situation often, but if you ever decide to model a crowd, you've got to approach painting the figures differently. The important thing is to paint only what will be seen.

This means completely painting only the figures around the periphery of a group, and painting only the sides of the figures that will be seen. People in the back of the throng can be painted as tops only, with simple dark bottoms to disguise the lack of attention.

POSING AND PAINTING FIGURES TO DIRECT ATTENTION

Little people can provide a spot of action in an otherwise static scene. I like to modify my figures and place them so they're involved in attention-getting poses.

Simple modifications to make them less recogniz-

able include figures pointing or gesturing and people operating vehicles or machinery. If you have several similar figures, just painting the shirts a different color goes a long way toward changing their look. Other simple changes are a new hat, a bald-headed man, black or oriental skin colors, placing figures on ladders, or figures handling something.

After I have a good variety of specially adapted figures I place them in little groups around the layout. A dull-looking street corner can be brought to life with a lady pushing her baby carriage, a small boy patting his dog, and several people waiting for the bus. Use your imagination!

MODIFYING FIGURES

It seems a bit grisly as I write about it, but chopping off and repositioning limbs is a great way to make figures distinctive and attention-getting. There's a certain amount of skill required to alter poses radically, but simple ones like rotating an arm at the shoulder so the engineer's hand reaches for the throttle are easy.

Amputations are even easier, though you shouldn't have more than two or three of them on your layout unless you want to be ghoulish. A one-armed man (the one who David Janssen was always looking for in "The Fugitive"); a fellow with a missing foot, perhaps on crutches; or an old sailor with a peg leg will add flavor and interest. If you model old-time railroading they're appropriate, too, because in the "good old days" being a railroader was even more dangerous an occupation than it is now.

DIFFERENT SCALES FOR FIGURES

If you spread out a variety of figures in almost any scale you'll find some are noticeably bigger. And the difference is not just tall or short. (Keep in mind that while people come in different sizes, the heads are usually about the same. One of the ways we spot tall people at a distance is to compare the size of the head to the rest of them.)

So what we've got is figures made to two or three different scales, and we can use this to advantage as a kind of forced perspective. For example, in HO, Preiser, Revell, and a couple of other European brands are accurately scaled, but Campbell (originally Weston), Atlas, and Lytler & Lytler brands are on the hefty side.

I like the slightly bigger-than-life figures because they draw attention to themselves, and they provide emphasis in foreground scenes. In a way, having the human element just a bit oversize is appropriate. After all, no matter how much you like trains, we're all people, and we're drawn to other people — even if they're only 1" tall!

MAKE UP A HANDY INSPECTOR GENERAL

For 30 years I've considered myself calibrated to HO scale, but sometimes I seem to forget what size I'm working in. This often happens when building and texturing scenery — I find myself making things too small, too vertically compressed or not high enough, because there's no handy reference to how tall everything really should be.

My solution is an "inspector general," a cheap HO unpainted figure mounted on a scrap of white styrene. Having him on the scene means I'm less likely to build things that don't look right because they're too short.

FIGURES IN YOUR VEHICLES

One of the most common criticisms of vehicles — including my own — is that they look stupid with

nobody behind the wheel. This is especially true of cars and trucks lined up at railroad grade crossings or (supposedly) rolling down the road.

The solution is easy: Chop up a few cheap plastic figures and install the upper portions in the drivers' seats of cars and trucks that ought to be occupied. Since the figures will most likely be in deep shadow, they can be the worst ones from your scrap box. In fact, what's needed here is silhouettes as much as anything.

KILLING THE SHINE
WITHOUT KILLING THE CAR

Real automobiles are are shiny, right, so why don't glossy car models look right on the layout? Well, think again: Up close real cars are indeed

glossy, but when you back off 40 or 50 feet (6" in HO scale), all but the shiniest cars show only a few highlight reflections.

I'm not a scientist, so I can't cite the precise physical reason why this is so, but a model phenomenon called "scale effect" means that things look different at varying distances. As you move away from an object, colors gray and seem to lighten and even a fire-engine shine gradually disappears. About the only thing that appears shiny at a distance is water, and its shine depends mostly on lighting.

So dull down your cars, trucks, and fire engines with a coat of clear flat finish, leaving only the glass areas to catch and reflect light. You can try a semi-gloss mixture of half-flat, half gloss on a car or two that you know will be in the foreground of your layout, but most of your vehicles should be dead flat, looking as if they need a good washing and waxing!

MAKING VEHICLES LOOK NATURAL

I can't ever imagine taking the time to make automobiles and trucks into moving models (hey, getting the trains to run is more than enough work!), but there are easy ways to make them look better while standing still.

Try opening a door and leaving it ajar for a car or truck that's stopped for loading. Pose a figure leaning on the vehicle, or about to get in or out. Turn the

front wheels to either side to make it look as if the car has just driven up, or open the hood and have a figure working inside, telling the story that something's gone wrong.

EASY-TO-MAKE HEADLIGHTS

An easy way to improve most off-the-shelf vehicles is to add a touch of sparkle with better headlights. The easiest (and cheapest!) way to make headlights is to coat the socket with silver paint, then follow up with a drop of two of Micro Krystal-Kleer after the paint dries. A quick sealing coat of clear gloss finish will keep the Krystal-Kleer from

clouding with time or minor humidity changes.

For a few foreground vehicles where the effect can really be noticed, try installing the appropriate size lens from MV Products. These foil-and-epoxy lenses are super realistic, and they catch available light to provide the look of a real lens and reflector.

FLATTEN THOSE TIRES!

The first trick that most aircraft and car modelers learn is to make a flat spot, sometimes with a side-

to-side bulge, on the bottoms of wheels to realistically simulate the weight of the machine. In smaller scales this is as simple as lightly stroking a completed vehicle across a sanding block to flatten the treads; in O and S you may want to use an old flatiron on medium heat to melt plastic or rubber tires. Sandwich a sheet of waxed paper between the tires and the iron to keep the melted plastic from sticking to the hot surface.

LOAD UP THOSE TRUCKS!

Scale trucks look a lot more purposeful when

there's something in the cargo bed. As long as the load has color and texture, it doesn't much matter what it is. Try stacking up oil drums (best ones on top, crummy ones at the bottom), or rusting up some surplus parts from plastic model airplane and military kits. Even a handful of colored stripwood bits from your scrapbox will add interest and dispel the look that the truck is a model instead of a hard-working machine.

CANVAS TEXTURE FOR TARPS AND COVERS

Facial tissue is the best stuff to simulate fabric texture such as tarps and cargo covers on trucks. Moisten a single or double thickness of the tissue with a mist of water, then drape it into place. While

it's wet, prod the tissue with a wet brush to introduce realistic folds and wrinkles. (If at first you don't succeed, scrap the attempt and try again — the raw material is literally disposable!)

When you like the way the tissue is draped use a brush to soak it with diluted white glue. Let the glue dry overnight, add a second coat if necessary, then paint the canvas with Polly S colors. Dry-brushing is mandatory to bring out the fabric texture.

VISORS FOR A SPORTY LOOK

Any modification you make to a familiar kit-built

vehicle is a big step toward making your layout different and unique. About the simplest one I've come up with is to graft a simple visor onto a vintage truck cab.

In HO scale it's sufficient to file a styrene strip to a triangular cross section, then glue it over the windshield; larger scales may require something more elaborate. Have you noticed that visors seem to be coming back on custom pickups and over-the-road trucks?

AMERICANIZING ASSEMBLED TRUCKS AND CARS

Vehicle collecting is a popular worldwide hobby, and that's one reason for the huge variety of HO and O scale vehicles. European brands like Viking and Herpa offer exquisite detail, but too often the cars have a distinctly foreign flavor. Also, their bright colors and glossy finishes don't look right on our carefully weathered railroads.

You can solve both problems at once, mostly with paint. The first step is to figure out the parts breakdown of each model, then carefully pry it apart. Some vehicles will snap apart; others will require grinding away assembly tabs or loosening joints with small applications of liquid plastic cement. Be especially careful with the cement around clear parts.

The next step is to modify the parts that make the car or truck clearly European. A Mercedes emblem is easy to spot and eliminate, as is a right-hand-drive steering wheel, and many modern European trucks have individual rounded fenders on the rear and trailer wheels that can simply be cut away to yield a more American look.

Put the clear parts aside and paint or Dullcote the body panels, frame, and detail parts, including any chromed parts. You'll be surprised how much difference simply painting the tires dark gray will make. When the paint has dried thoroughly (I like a couple of days, maybe more), apply a thinned burnt umber or black oil wash, and let dry.

Finish the paint job with a light coat of Testor's Dullcote, followed by light dry-brushing with Polly S antique white or earth, then reassemble the parts.

FUN WITH CHEAP KIT VEHICLES

Vehicles vary in quality, but that doesn't mean you can't use all those appropriate for your scale and era. Put the best ones down front and the weaker ones further away. Often the trick is to take the cruder vehicles and pose them with their backs to the camera or viewer.

I'm thinking particularly of a couple of HO plastic structure kits that included vehicles, and of one or two brands that were very inexpensive — and worth what they cost.

Instead of consigning these models to the trash, have some fun with them. Background areas, where the poor proportions of lack of detail won't be noticed, are a natural place to put them to work, but how about modeling them as burned-out hulks in a junkyard, or sawing them up and having only the back or front half protruding from a loading door or alley? You're much less likely to worry about sawing up rough models than a costly detailed kit, and that means you can have more fun with them.

EASY TWO-TONE PAINT JOBS

A two-tone paint job is a great way to customize a built-up automobile, and such schemes were common until the early 1960s. You don't have to paint

both colors; instead, cover various panels with a paint-on liquid mask, paint the contrasting color, then remove the masking and apply Dullcote. The base color of vehicle becomes the second color. Be sure to emphasize the car's cast-in color separation lines with brown or black wash, or chrome trim.

CHROME TRIM

Chromed plastic parts are way too toylike to look good in scale, so it's best to paint over them with silver paint. Try using a paint pencil — a felt-tip marker filled with silver paint — to pick out fine chrome strips, or combine a steady hand with a fine paintbrush. You can find such pencils at art supply or craft stores, and a few have been offered specifically for hobby use, including a good one from Tamiya.

SHIMS FOR GLUING WHEELS

Every vehicle should sit level on its wheels, but some kits don't provide an accurate way to position individual wheels on the frame or body. When this happens to you, place scraps of sheetwood or styrene underneath the body to hold it level, then glue on the wheels. I use a slow-setting adhesive like 5-minute epoxy to give me time to adjust the wheels one by one.

WHEELS THAT WON'T FIT

When you run into a model where the wheels won't fit up into the wheel wells, try cutting off the top of wheel instead of laboriously grinding away the body. You'll save time, and the missing portion of the tire will never be seen — or missed.

PREPPING SOLID CARS AND TRUCKS

Solid cast vehicles such as the Magnuson (Walthers) HO cars and trucks will benefit from an extra touch before painting. After cleaning up the castings with files and sandpaper, I give the body a vigorous scrubbing with tooth powder and an old toothbrush to prepare it for priming and painting.

The mild abrasive seems to work away the rough edges and make the vehicles smoother, eliminating some of the rawness of the polyester casting process.

WINDSHIELD DETAIL
THAT ISN'T THERE

Whether your model has windhield wipers or not, you can imply the detail by showing the area of the glass that the wiper should have wiped. Cut a pie-wedge-shaped piece of masking tape to cover the swept area, then airbrush the car with Dullcote. Remove the tape, and presto! — the wipers must've been working during that last rain!

ADDING STATE LICENSE PLATES

They're probably the tiniest details on my layout, but I've added license plates to most of my vehicles.

I use simple bits of Evergreen 1x6 about 12 scale inches long, and I chose yellow for Maine in 1941, even though I don't know what color the real plates were that year.

The important feature here is that the license plates add spots of bright color, and having most of them the same implies that the layout is indeed located somewhere.

FENDER SKIRTS

Remember those great '59 Cadillacs, the ones with the rear fender skirts that covered up most of the wheel? (If you ever had to change a flat tire on one, that was a different story!) Adding fender skirts to a vintage car is an easy way to make it different from the stock kit. Make a simple insert from styrene sheet, glue it into the opening, then fair over it with filler putty, sand smooth, prime, and paint.

What a lineup of vintage HO iron — and not a "For Sale" sign on one of them! Those tiny yellow license plates add a bright spot of color to each of these vehicles, and making the color all the same tells your viewer that the cars and trucks all hail from the same state or province.

After the fanciful stone station at Head Tide grabs the viewer's attention, it's the job of the station agent's rose trellis to draw him into the scene and keep his attention there.

6
Detailing and superdetailing

Focusing interest on your layout with things to see

ALL DETAILING DEPENDS ON the viewer. Often, that viewer will be you, but you should pretend otherwise; you should think through your scenes and calculate the effects you want to achieve in the mind of someone who's seeing your layout for the first time. Then, weeks, months, or even years after you first build a scene, you may be able to return to it fresh and see if it works!

Once you've settled on how you want to focus the viewer's interest and what you want him to see, think in terms of zones. An obvious division is near and far: Areas close to the viewer naturally rate more detail than those in the background. But it isn't always that simple — if you have an interesting scene beyond arm's reach, a roundhouse, for example, you may want to intentionally keep the foreground in front of it plain so your viewer is drawn to the focal point.

Once you've decided where and what to detail, here are a couple of dozen tips on how to do it.

SAY IT WITH FLOWERS

Adding a rose trellis or a couple of flower boxes to one of your buildings is easy, and it's a detail you won't find on every layout you visit. The trellis can be a simple fan of small styrene or wood strips; the flower box doesn't have to be a box at all — just paint a length of stripwood and glue a few tufts of brightly colored ground foam texture to the top edge.

You can use these touches of color to draw the viewer's eye to something you particularly want him to see, but don't be too cute too often. A touch of whimsy here and there is great, but remember that a little goes a long way.

PICKING OUT DETAIL WITH DABS OF COLOR

Small detail items such as tools will show up a lot

better in highly detailed, textured scenes if they are painted in bright colors — yellow, red, orange, and strong blues or greens. Tiny lobster buoys on a waterfront scene or logging tools in the woods will blend into the texture and undergrowth if you don't make them stand out with strong colors. You can still weather over the bright hues, but the basic idea of using them to catch a viewer's eye will be accomplished.

You can use a simple variation of the same trick to imply that there's detail where there's actually none at all. For example, a plain, undetailed dashboard on a car can be dressed up with a few white dots to imply detailed gauges that aren't there! Try it!

MASS-PAINTING DETAIL PARTS

Most of us paint detail parts a few at a time, usually when they're furnished with a kit. If you're between kits, though, try painting 50 or 100 barrels, crates, tires, or other details for use around your layout or next diorama. You'll save time in the long run, and gradually your layout will accumulate a rich "crust" of detail items.

Clean up the parts with sanding sticks and files, rinse away dirt and oils with a quick bath in denatured alcohol, then set them up on scrap cardboard-and-masking-tape flats for painting. I like to sort the parts according to the base color they'll be painted, and I try to paint six or more colors in a session.

Airbrush the parts, starting with light colors and progressing to darker ones. Then allow the paint to dry for a week or more (a good time to get started on a new modeling project!) before picking out details with contrasting colors and applying weathering treatments. Finish up with dry-brushing, then go looking for places to glue them down. You'll be amazed at how quickly a layout or even a small scene can absorb detail — but the result is always increased realism.

MAKING 55-GALLON DRUMS INTERESTING

Railroading is an industrial activity that serves other industries, so you'll need a lot of oil drums on your layout. You can make them more interesting by varying colors. Try painting the lids or middle bands a bright contrasting color, and add small bits of decals or paper labels on foreground drums. Try denting a few of the drums with a soldering iron before painting, too, but only a few.

PUT TRASH IN THOSE BARRELS!

Most of the barrels you see on layouts or dioramas are capped, but Grandt line makes HO and O scale hollow oil drums and wood barrels, and the old Revell HO structure kits included empty barrels. To vary their look, fill a few barrels and drums with trash, sticks, ground foam, or dirt. They'll be evidence that somebody's been cleaning up, and just a bit of added realism.

MAKING THE MOST OF CRUDE DETAIL

No brands mentioned, but kits occasionally include relatively crude detail parts. Even if the parts are substandard you can make them into excellent supporting players on your layout with careful painting followed by a dark wash and dry-brushing. Be sure to pick out molded details with bright colors before applying weathering treatments.

Then add the rough details to your layout where they'll be a foot or more from the front edge, or, if you need them up front, partially bury them in sand or vegetation. Placing top-notch detail parts in front of the rough ones will help convince viewers that everything is best-quality.

LADING PILES AND BINS

Visible volumes of important cargoes help establish the purpose for your railroad by showing what it carries. These can range from a parking lot full of

new cars with a spur track of auto racks nearby, to stacks of logs and lumber at a sawmill, to piles of coal, sand, pulpwood, gravel, or grain.

The important thing is to make the piles as big as you can — many railroads started out as single-purpose conveyor belts built to move a specific lading. If you're going to operate a convincing conveyor belt, you'd better have plenty of cargo for it to convey.

MODELING STAINS AND SPILLS

Nothing perks up a scene more than an accident that just happened. One of the easiest to stage is a spill. I staged an accident showing spilled apples in front of a general store, using boxes full of apples and an empty box from S.S. Ltd. The loose apples are fine lead shot used to weight locomotives, painted red and spread near the tipped box.

Another spill idea that's easy to model is melting ice. Just paint a trail of gloss varnish or acrylic gloss medium so that it runs downhill and looks natural.

MAKING LADING PILES

You don't have to waste a whole bag of expensive texture material to make a big pile of sand or coal. Instead, try this: Cut a circle of paper or light cardboard and make a slit from one edge to the center. Form it into a paper cone of approximately the right slope for the material you intend to pile up, then glue it to the layout.

Slowly add loose texture over the paper cone and bond it in place with dilute matte medium or white glue. Do this in several steps so you don't soak the cone and collapse it.

PEGS FOR FREE-STANDING DETAILS

Tall, free-standing items like gas pumps, phone poles, and even trees in exposed foreground loca-

tions are good candidates to be pinned into the scenery instead of glued. The idea is to cement a length of $\frac{1}{32}$" or larger wire into the base of the detail part, then drill a corresponding hole in the layout. Touching a colored marker to the scenery around the hole will help you find it.

Making the detail removable means you can pick it off before cleaning the layout or working on the surrounding area. And if a careless elbow hits the part, chances are you can re-bend the pin and drop the detail back into place — without having to dig it out of the scenery.

SURVIVABILITY FOR DELICATE DETAILS

A few years back I found some dandy photoetched brass weathervanes, and if they're not on the mar-

ket now, you could easily cut something convincing out of thin styrene sheet. Trouble is, no matter what you make it from, a weathervane in any scale is going to be pretty fragile, and by its very nature it's going to be in harm's way. (Trust me on this — I learned it the hard way.)

My solution is to make delicate details removable wherever possible, so they can be safely stored off the layout most of the time and dropped into place

for visitors' day or photos. Make the post of the weathervane a loose fit in its hole in the structure roof, and add a round bead below the flat parts to keep it from dropping too far into its socket.

SIMPLE DETAILS ADD UP

Occasionally you'll want to use a plain model in the foreground where you should have maximum detail. A simple way to bring a bare-bones accessory or building up to snuff is to spruce it up by applying nut-bolt-washer castings and a variety of styrene circles, squares, and rectangles.

The photo shows a dockside crane made from an inexpensive British kit that has been given this treatment. As it came out of the box it was pretty much a plain-Jane item; with an assortment of simple add-on details, most of them just bits of Evergreen styrene strips, it became a focal point in an important scene.

THE CHEAPEST DETAIL YOU'LL EVER FIND

The next time the mailman brings a particularly big wad of junk mail, grab your scissors and cut a few dozen rectangles of various colors of paper from the envelopes. Make them about 9" x 12" in your scale, but vary the sizes and don't be fussy.

Now head for the layout for a littering spree. Glue the paper bits in foreground areas where you'd be likely to find waste paper: between tracks, in streets and gutters, and around trash piles. I keep a Zip-Loc bag of these scrap-paper bits with my scenic texture materials, and I occasionally use them as labels on crates and barrels, too.

. . . AND JUST AS INEXPENSIVE

Leftover board ends and bits of stripwood make good trackside detail. When you finish a wood kit,

chop up the scraps that are too small to save, stain them weathered gray, and glue them in appropriate spots. You'll always find board ends and lumber scraps around industrial spurs and yard tracks.

ACCENTING WITH SCENIC TEXTURE

We've all learned to paint models down with dulled colors and weathering so they don't look bright and toylike, but like other good things, too much of this can make for a dull scene. In one instance where I realized I'd done this, I experimented with using colorful scenic textures to subtly spice up the area immediately surrounding the structure. I was surprised and pleased with the result.

The idea is to texture and color the area just as you usually would, then add small amounts of colorful ground foam or dirt texture as accents here and

there. I used some relatively bright red Western dirt and sand around a stamp mill, and it worked; colorful flowers or perhaps a tree laden with bright red apples would do the same for an understated dwelling or store.

MODELING BARBED WIRE

If you're into country-and-western modeling and want to effectively model those wide-open spaces, you need barbed-wire fences. I make barbed wire on the workbench using 8 lb. test monofilament fishing line. I tie a knot in the monofilament every scale 24" to represent the barbs twisted on the wire.

To facilitate the knot tying, I made a barbed wire fence jig with seven headless pins pushed into the jig 24" apart (if you have lots of patience make a jig with 30 pins — your fence making will go faster). The jig also has holes to space the fence poles correctly, to

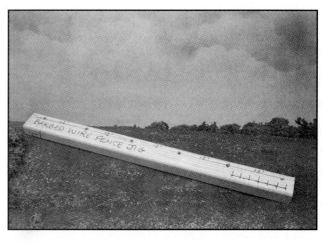

set the posts at the correct depth, and to space the barbed wire on the pole.

Start the fence by cutting a 2' length of monofilament and tie an overhand knot close to one end. Slip the knot over the right-most pin and pull it tight. Working to the left, tie a loose overhand knot around the next pin and pull tight. Repeat until all the pins have knots on them.

Slip the knots from the pins and pull tight. Hold the last knot next to the right hand pin and repeat the knot-tying process. Repeat the knot tying until you have enough barbed wire for your fence. Now color the barbed wire with Polly S Stainless Steel paint and weather it with a wash of Rustall.

Typical barbed wire fences are 4'6" high and consist of either three or four strands spaced 10" to 16" apart. Three-strand fences look best.

Make fence posts from stained 4x4 stripwood cut 7' long. These posts are placed in the scenery on 12' to 15' centers and this is where the jig comes in handy. Just set the jig where the fence posts will go and poke the holes through the jig using an awl. Put a drop of white glue on each post and push into place.

The strands of barbed wire are fastened to the posts using super glue, keeping the wire tight during installation. I tie one end of the monofilament to the

first post, add a drop of super glue, and let it set. I pull the mono past the last post and apply a clamp-type weight to the end of the line so that it pulls the line tight. Apply a drop of glue where the line crosses each post. Repeat until you have the three lines parallel to each other.

After I finished making a demonstration fence I found it easier to cut every other tooth from a comb to make a knot-tying jig.

USING FENCES

One of the best way to separate scenes on your layout is with fences. Fences provide an acceptable boundary line and can make small areas on the layout look larger. A fence at the rear of the layout can serve as a divider separating the foreground from the background. Even short bits of fence left over from other projects can be used alongside a structure. The fences on my layout are evenly divided between being heavily weathered and plastered with signs, and those that are just painted, Tom Sawyer-looking. White picket fences, especially, give the scene a turn-of-the-century look.

Central Valley offers a good-looking assortment of HO scale fences (No. 1601). These are injection-molded plastic and can be painted while still attached to the sprue. Several European structure manufacturers include fences in their kits. And, when all else fails, a great-looking board fence can be made in minutes from a sheet of scribed wood.

A SHARP WAY TO
INSTALL PHONE POLES!

Getting phone poles to stay straight and not loosen in the scenery can be a real problem, espe-

cially if you have lots of them. A friend showed me a quick and easy way to keep the poles tight in their holes. He puts a point on the bottom of each pole in a pencil sharpener, then forces the pole into an undersized hole drilled into the scenery. There's no need for glue, and the taper on the bottom of the pole wedges it firmly in place.

PIRATING DETAILS
THAT WON'T BE SEEN

A lot of us build kit structures while we're between layouts, when we can't be sure which sides will be visible. I've always spread the detail parts pretty evenly over such buildings, just to make them pleasing individual models as I build each one.

When it comes time to install such buildings in a scene, I make it a practice to break off details that won't be seen for use elsewhere on the layout. It's a simple thing, but it can make a difference — and no scene or layout has enough detail!

CHOOCH JUNKYARD JUNK

An absolute treasure trove of great detail is to be found in two products in the HO Chooch line. Called "Junk Piles," each provides a couple of heaps of scrap metal, and the automotive set even includes several rotting car chassis.

The polyurethane castings are designed to be plunked down on your layout, and the scenery worked up to the edges. That'll work fine, but you can get a lot more mileage out of them by cutting the heaps into smaller piles, picking out a few parts with brightly colored paints, and thinning down the edges before working them into your layout. (Watch out for the urethane dust when sawing or sanding. I seem to be allergic to it, and it irritates me so much that the only way I'll work with it is outdoors on a breezy day. I also give the castings a generous spray coat of Floquil Railroad Colors paint, which seems to seal in the chemical smell.)

PAINT THAT PLASTIC TRACK!

Plastic track — either sectional or flex-track — can look every bit as good as hand-laid with a little painting. You can paint it before spiking or nailing it down or after it's all in place, but before ballasting.

I prefer the latter, since soldering rail joints is easier when you don't have to clean paint off the rail ends.

Either way, load up your airbrush with a nondescript gray-brown mixture (I prefer Floquil Railroad Colors for this job, though I've used Accu-Flex with good results). I like a combination of roughly 25 percent Grimy Black, 25 percent Earth, and 50 percent Rail Brown. Spray the track sections, but don't worry about perfect coverage because the next step is to add more Earth to the paint mix and randomly spray side-to-side to vary the colors of the individual ties.

Finish spraying by mixing a little of your overall color into a lot of Grime, and again hit a few random ties with a side-to-side motion. Then roughly dry-brush the ties with Polly S Earth applied with a 1" brush, polish the rail tops and inside edges with a Bright Boy track-cleaning block, and you're ready for ballast.

PAINTING RAIL TO MAKE IT LOOK SMALLER

One of the great myths in model railroading is all the concern expressed over the years about rail size. The model railroad magazines have spilled gallons of ink and spent hours hand-wringing over the idea that we need smaller — much smaller — rail. In HO narrow gauge circles, this ultimately led to Code 40 rail, which looks good but is virtually impractical for building an operating model railroad.

A far better solution is to paint oversize rail a dark color to make it look smaller. My favorite color has always been Flo-Paque Burnt Umber, but they don't make it any more. Instead, I use a half-and-half mixture of Floquil Rail Brown and Roof Brown. Apply the paint with a No. 1 brush only to the side of the rails that your viewers will see, let it set one hour, then polish the top and inside edges of rail with a Bright Boy abrasive block.

You'll be pleasantly surprised at how this simple technique makes the rail look much smaller — and when you get used to it, unpainted rail looks downright naked. (Real rail isn't bright silver, so unpainted rail on a beautifully detailed model railroad is utterly unrealistic.)

USE SMALL RAIL IN THE FOREGROUND

If you're going to use really light rail (Code 40, 55, or 60) anywhere on your layout, use it on a few spur tracks in the foreground. Since viewers will see this rail first (and best), it helps convey the impression that all the rail is light. Using larger rail on the main line helps establish that the main is more important, and using sturdier rail in the background of the railroad is smart because it's easier to work with and maintain than the light stuff.

MAGIC WANDS FOR CLEANING TRACK

What are we doing talking about track cleaning in a book on detailing? Well, the more detailed your layout becomes, the tougher it is to clean the rails without wiping out trackside details. Your big old ham fist with a full-sized Bright Boy abrasive block is just too clunky to reach into a lot of scenes, but we want that highly detailed layout to run, too.

The solution is to mount chunks of Bright Boys on various handles, which I call "Bright Boy on a Stick."

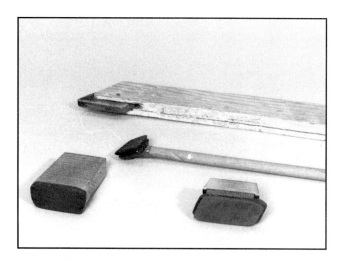

about the simplest: a sledlike sliding Masonite pad mounted on a couple of nails that protrude into the floor of the car. Legendary modeler John Allen used these sliders on his layout, and judging from the amount of black crud they pick up on my railroad, they do a great job.

You'll need a few scraps of $^1/_8$" tempered Masonite, the hard kind. The smooth-one-side variety is best, but you can use the kind that's smooth on both sides by scuffing the side that will ride the rails with coarse sandpaper. Cut a rectangle of Masonite about $^1/_4$" wider than your track, and from $1^1/_4$" (N gauge or HOn3) to 2" long (HO or S). Bevel the bottom (rough side) at both ends with a sanding block so it won't catch on switch points or minor vertical glitches in the track.

Chuck a 1" box nail in your motor tool or electric drill and file the head flat. While you're at it, smooth the shank of the nail, then cut it off about $^3/_4$" from the head. Make two nails for each slider, and glue them to the top of the sliding pad on the centerline, $^3/_4$" to 1" apart. I use 5-minute epoxy or a gap-filling super glue for this.

When the glue has cured, hold the nails against the centerline of the car you've chosen to carry the slider, mark the locations, and drill matching holes. Make the holes about $^1/_{32}$" over-size: You want the nails completely free to slide up and down as the Masonite pad slides its way smoothly

My favorite is mounted at a 45-degree angle on the end of an 18" length of $^1/_2$" dowel, perfect for reaching into bridges, tunnel mouths, and between buildings. Another handy one is super-glued to the bottom of a $^1/_2$" x $1^1/_2$" wood block, which gets your hand up high enough off the track to avoid bashing details.

JOHN ALLEN'S SLIDER TRACK CLEANING CARS

The best way to clean the main line on your layout without knocking down details is to run your trains. Simply barreling along with an engine and half a dozen cars helps knock dust off the rails, but running cars with some sort of track cleaner underneath does an even better job.

Over the years there have been all sorts of commercial cleaning cars, some with pads to dispense track-cleaning fluid onto the rails, and others to wipe it off. But the most successful design is just

and efficiently along the rails, cleaning as it goes.

Insert the nails into their holes and place the car on the rails. Now simply run it in your trains, and watch how much black stuff it picks up. Remove the pad from the car from time to time and clean the bottom surface by rubbing it on a coarse sanding block. (If you haven't run the trains for a while, try pushing one of these slider cars ahead of the engine to knock the worst of the dirt off the rails.)

INVISIBLE TRACK CLEANING CARS

Over the years I've stumbled across a couple of

commercial track cleaning cars I liked, but they were strictly business — they didn't look like realistic scale rolling stock. I disguised them by building a boxcar body around one and a snowplow superstructure over the other. Now I can run the cars in trains anytime I want, and no one notices them, not even me.

MAKE MINE CLEAN, DRY TRACK

One of the minor ongoing controversies in model railroading concerns using hair-clipper oil or some other preparation as a non-oxidant coating on the rail heads. The oil proponents theorize that the coating prevents arcing and sparking, which keeps the track from pitting.

Mark me down on the side of the dry-track faction. While I've noted over the years that my layouts run better in summertime, when there's more moisture in the air and less dust being blown around by the hot-air furnace, my experience with liquid on the rails has been anything but good.

Oil, contact-cleaner fluid, or anything else I've tried on the rails has simply made itself into a hard, nonconductive paintlike crud. While I like to use contact cleaner (off the layout) to remove the unavoidable black stuff from locomotive wheels, the best approach for track cleaning is to run the trains — with the kind of cleaner cars described above — as often as you can, and use oil only for lubrication.

The train is clearly the most important element in this scene — it's supposed to be! But look again, and note how the colorful signs beyond engine No. 14 help draw your eye up the street.

7

Signs of life

Telling your story the obvious way — with words and pictures

WALK DOWN MAIN STREET and try to count the signs; you'll give up before you make it to the end of the first block! The commercial messages bombard you with information — usually what to buy or where to eat — while street, traffic, and safety signs show you how to get there and keep order. Signs pop up everywhere, and every one of them provides an easily understood message that your railroad serves a busy human population.

ESTABLISHING YOUR ERA WITH SIGNS

Your railroad should tell a story, and you have to provide as many clues as you can to establish its setting — especially where and when. The "when" part — your era — is a difficult concept for non-model-railroad visitors to understand, and one of the best ways to put it across is with signs.

Advertising signs for well-known commercial products — automobiles, soft drinks, gasoline, and soap,

to name a few — are especially good for this. Decal and detail-part manufacturers have offered sign sets tagged to specific periods, and they are a great place to start. MODEL RAILROADER also occasionally prints period signs in the magazine. You may have to research to determine exactly when a certain company used a logo or slogan, but that's just part of the fun!

MAKING STATION SIGNS TO IDENTIFY YOUR LOCALE

Station signs are important in establishing the key place names on your railroad, and I've always been willing to put in some extra time to make them better than just OK.

The first thing to decide on is a standard color scheme. If you're modeling a prototype railroad a bit of research is in order to determine the right color combination; if you free-lance, adopting your own scheme will enhance your railroad's identity. If you want to use a computer laser printer for the signs

you'll usually be stuck with black and white, but I'd suggest something more colorful. My own favorite: white letters on a medium-blue background.

In recent years computer typesetting has become common and inexpensive, and if it's available to you it's a good choice, particularly if you can obtain color output. For most of the signs on my layout, though, I use dry-transfer alphabet letters applied one at a time.

Paint a swatch of styrene sheet with your background color, let it dry for a couple of days, then tape it to a sheet of graph paper to serve as an alignment aid. Write down the station names you plan to make on a sheet of scratch paper, and check the spelling against a map or dictionary. (Nothing's worse than spending an evening making a pair of beautiful station signs, only to discover a spelling error at 11 p.m.)

Now establish a baseline for the letters and begin applying the characters at the center of the sign. Work from the middle out toward the ends, burnishing down each letter when you're satisfied with its alignment. When a letter goes down crooked or improperly spaced, pick it off with a swatch of Scotch Magic Tape or masking tape. This is important, and

a willingness to do it over until you get it right is the main ingredient in top-notch signmaking.

Note that all letters in the alphabet don't take up the same amount of space: Ms are fat, Is are skinny. Round and slant-sided letters like O, G, A, and V should be moved closer to adjacent characters; vertical, straight-sided letters like M, N, and H are placed farther apart. Use a photo of a prototype sign or a reference like a magazine headline as a guide for eyeballing the correct pleasing spacings.

When you're happy with the lettering, burnish the transfers down one more time and cut the sign out of the sheet. Paint the edges, then spray the sign with clear flat finish and add it to your depot. Even if the depot is a rambling wreck, don't weather the sign: Lack of weathering will make the signboard "pop out" at your visitors, which is exactly the effect you want!

PAINTING SIGNS ON BUILDINGS — I

Signs painted right on your buildings lend a distinctive look to your layout. The new computers with laser printers offer a great way to come up with these. (If you don't have access to one of these computers, you probably know someone who does. Many instant print shops offer the use of one as a service.)

Start by setting the wording you want for the sign in a variety of sizes and typefaces (fonts). This is quick and easy to do. When you come up with a size and style that looks good, set it in the "outline" style, which gives you a thin line around the outside of the letters.

Now print out the type on the laser printer and use the outlines to cut a stencil with a sharp, new, No. 10 X-acto knife blade, the one with the rounded nose. Leave connecting bridges to position the insides of Os, Ds, Bs, and other letters with captured middles.

Fasten the stencil to the building with a light coat of rubber cement and clean up any cement that gets into the letter areas with a rubber cement pickup from your art store. Then mask the rest of the building with plastic wrap and airbrush the color of the lettering. Spray through the stencil only at a 90-degree angle so the paint won't get under the edges.

Remove the stencil right away and clean up the rubber cement residue. Touch up the parts of the letters that were covered by the stencil bridges, carefully scrape away excess paint, and weather the sign along with the rest of the building.

A variation on this technique is to find a prototype building with a sign that you like, shoot a straight-on (preferably telephoto) photo of it, then carefully enlarge the shot to your scale and use the photo print to make the stencil mask. The elaborate front on the Smith Bros. Fish building was made this way.

PAINTING SIGNS ON BUILDINGS — II

A slightly-more-difficult way to make painted-on signs is to make your own decals. I had to use this on a coal bunker where the framing was on the outside, preventing me from using a stencil.

Make the lettering as described above, then cut out individual letters and rubber-cement them to the building to be sure you like the size and shape. Next, remove the paper letters and use them as cutting templates for decals.

I sprayed white Floquil on a sheet of old white decals, let it dry for a day, then coated the paint with Micro-Scale Super Film to strengthen it. Then I rubber-cemented individual letters to the decal sheet and cut out each with scissors and a sharp knife.

Apply the individual decal letters to the building, using repeated applications of decal solvent to make them snuggle down into the surface. The sign will look so good that people will ask how you did it!

PAINTING SIGNS ON BUILDINGS — III

Painting a sign directly on a building wall makes a great-looking eye catcher, and it's easier to do than you might think. I dressed up a tall bank building in my waterfront-city scene with a "Down East Bank of MAINE" sign that goes a long way toward establishing the setting for my visitors. Here's how.

Mask the side of the building and paint the area

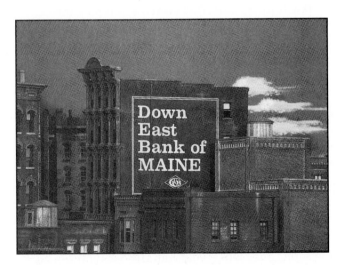

of the sign white (or other light color, but white is the most common). Let this dry thoroughly (a week is a good bet), and while it dries head off to your art-supply store to find an appropriate set of dry-transfer lettering to make the sign. I used Chartpak 60-point Clarendon Bold on the bank.

Now burnish down the letters over the white

background. You can get fancy here: I added a 1/16"-wide white border stripe made with strips of masking tape. When the lettering is the way you want it, airbrush over it with black or some other dark color.

Let the paint dry for half an hour, then lift off the tape and dry transfers by pressing over them with masking tape. It may take repeated tries, but eventually the transfer film will lift, revealing crisp white letters. Touch up with a fine brush, let the dark color dry for a week, then weather the signs along with the surrounding wall. Presto!

BETTER SIGNS WITH DRY TRANSFERS

I like dry transfer signs because most are brighter and more colorful than paper signs. But some modelers won't use dry transfers, mostly because the

transfers often don't release completely from their backing — half the sign transfers properly to the model, while the other half remains stuck to its carrier sheet.

Hold the transfer near an incandescent light bulb for about 15 seconds, then immediately rub it on the model to get a 100 percent transfer every time. To set the signs and make them permanent, put a drop of MEK (methyl-ethyl-ketone) or another solvent-type styrene cement next to the transfer. Capillary action will draw the MEK under the transfer, softening it, and it will settle into the structure siding. Don't touch the transfer while it's wet — it's soft and will distort or tear. After the solvent dries the transfer can be weathered just like a paper sign.

HOW TO APPLY DECALS

Everybody knows the ins and outs of applying decals, right? Well, maybe not, judging from the questions I've fielded over the years. Once you've got the knack of it — and a workable system with the right combination of setting solutions — working with decals becomes second nature (and easy). I use a six-step process.

1. Gloss coat the model. The first step doesn't have much to do with the decals themselves, but everything to do with how well they'll go on. Each decal marking consists of a layer of clear film with the markings painted on the top and a water-soluble adhesive on the bottom. The adhesive-and-film sandwich will pull itself down tightly to a smooth glossy surface, but it won't adhere to a flat surface worth a darn, so you have to apply a glossy coating to the areas where the decals will go.

Why not use glossy paint, add the decals, then apply a flat finish? Well, this will work, but it means painting more of the model, and I find that it's harder to see what I'm doing working on a glossy-painted surface. I prefer to lightly airbrush only those spots where the decals will go with Floquil Crystal-Coat. There's no need to mask — just spray the clear gloss coating over the flat paint.

2. Trim the decals. A few brands of decals offer a no-trim type of film, where the film is applied only directly under the markings, but most have a complete sheet of film with the markings printed over it. This means you'll need to cut out each marking, eliminating as much of the surrounding film as possible.

I use fine-pointed cuticle scissors to trim off the film, and a magnifying visor is helpful. As I trim each piece from the sheet I arrange it where it will go on the model. You'll be surprised how much this simple step helps in visualizing how the completed sign will look, and it's a whole lot easier to slide the decal sections around while they're still dry.

3. Soak and apply. Now choose the first piece of decal and drop it onto a shallow pan of water to soak it off the backing. Most decals will curl as the water soaks the backing paper, then relax back to flat. As soon as the decal goes back to flat, remove it from the water and set it on a clean piece of paper towel to wick away most of the water.

Quickly apply a drop or two of MicroScale Micro-Set solution to the model where the marking will go. Micro-Set is a dilute acetic acid solution, and acts as a wetting agent to help the decal film slide onto the surface without trapping air bubbles. Nothing else works as well.

Place the decal, with backing paper, over the drop of Micro-Set and gently slide the backing paper out from under the film. If you can see air bubbles, add a couple of drops of Micro-Set and slide the film around until they're gone. Then position the decal exactly where it belongs and use a small block of soft foam rubber to gently press it into the surface. Wick away most of the Micro-Set with a torn scrap of paper towel. Repeat the process until you've applied all the decal pieces to one section of the model

(usually, a single side or wall).

4. Soften and conform. When the decal has almost dried, say, about 20 minutes, you can start applying solvent setting solution. This actually softens and dissolves the backing film, allowing it to settle down over recessed and raised detail on the model. Apply the first few drops of solution (I like MicroScale Micro-Sol) cautiously with a brush around the edges of each marking, allowing the liquid to seep in under the film by capillary action.

If the solvent setting solution makes the decal wrinkle up, leave it alone: It will settle back down as the solvent dries. After your first couple of applications have dried, you can apply the solvent in heavier coats, brushing it liberally over the surface of the markings. Gradually — I've used as many as 20 applications — the solvent will snuggle the decal down against the surface.

5. For stubborn markings. Decals vary, and while most will settle down easily, every now and then you'll find a stinker. The first thing to try is a stronger setting solvent: Walthers Solvaset is slightly stronger than Micro-Set, or if you're really daring you can try a drop or two of full-strength denatured alcohol.

If the film refuses to settle down, chuck up a brand-new No. 11 blade in your X-acto knife and make light cuts through the film. This is especially effective where the decal needs to settle down into grooves between siding boards. Then apply setting solvent to make the cut film conform to the underlying contours.

6. Cleanup and flat coating. Steps 1 through 4 can be accomplished one after another, but after the final application of solvent it's best to allow the decals to dry overnight. Then use a Q-Tip dampened with water to gently swab away any stains visible around the markings. Let this dry for at least an hour before overcoating the decals and surrounding area with Testor Dullcote or Floquil Clear Flat Finish. Dullcote is my favorite, but whatever you use, don't skimp. A medium-heavy coat of flat will cover the decal and blend it into the surrounding surface of the model.

I like to let the flat finish dry for a week or more before weathering over the decals, just to be safe.

FOR DECALS THAT WON'T STICK

Sometimes when you soak the decal off the backing paper it simply won't stick: The adhesive that's supposed to do the job has gone bad.

If the marking is intact, try mixing a solution of one part white glue to five parts water, dip the decal in it, then apply it to the model. Blot away excess glue solution with a bit of torn paper towel, then use setting solutions to soften up the decal as usual.

FOR DECALS THAT EXPLODE

Unlike people, decals don't age well. Changes in humidity are particularly bad for the carrier film, and old decals often explode — when you drop a decal section into water to soak it off the backing, the film and markings simply fall apart.

Micro-Scale decals are particularly susceptible to this sort of failure, so it's appropriate that Micro-Scale offers a product to repair old, delicate, or dried-out decals: Micro Super Film. Brush a generous coat of the film over the face of the decals while still on the backing sheet, let dry, cut out, and apply as usual. In a pinch a heavy coat of clear flat or gloss will rehabilitate old decals, but Micro Super Film is my product of choice.

DECALS ON THE INSIDE

To hide the film on decals provided for storefront windows, apply them face-side-to on the inside of the glazing material. If the decals don't seem to have enough stickum on their faces to adhere to the clear

plastic, dip them in a solution of three parts water to one part white glue before working them into place. Usually, you won't need to use decal-setting solution.

A DECAL SIGN KIT YOU MAY NOT KNOW ABOUT

A few years back (for me that usually means 10 years ago) Walthers introduced an HO sign kit, and because I haven't seen it in use on as many layouts as I expected it's worth mentioning here.

Walthers No. 941-3136 HO sign set consists of more than a dozen molded styrene signboards and about two dozen decals to apply to them. The decal sheet also provides another two dozen or so signs to be applied to the inside of storefront windows.

The key in using this sign set is to paint the plastic frames a variety of base and trim colors, then apply

the decals. I start by airbrushing the plastic sprue with white, then brush paint the edges. After a light coat of clear gloss the decals go on easily, followed by clear flat and weathering treatments.

IMPROVING BLACK-AND-WHITE SIGNS

When I visit layouts I see a lot of black-and-white signs. Sure, there are plenty of such signs out there in the real world, but there's a lot of color too. It's easy to spruce up simple printed signs (often made on a copy machine or laser printer) with transparent colors.

Try adding color to these signs by coloring lettering or border areas with see-through markers and highlighters. For a wider selection of colors, try Dr. P.H. Martin's transparent dyes, available at art supply stores.

MAKING LASER-PRINTED SIGNS

Nowadays a lot of folks have access to a desktop computer and a laser printer, and if you do you're all set to make your own black-and-white signs. Just boot up your favorite word processing or desktop-publishing program and go to it.

Most programs allow you to type the words that will appear on the sign, then adjust the font (type style) and size to exactly the way you want it to print

out. Some programs will also let you draw a box, or several nested boxes, around the type, to provide borders and simplify cutting out the sign.

Print out the sign, check it for size or type style, then make a final print. Glue the sign to cardboard and color it with markers, then mount it on your building and weather it along with the rest of the structure.

COPY THOSE SIGNS

Well-known modeler George Sellios is famous for the spectacular signs on the city buildings on his Franklin & South Manchester. For a decade he's

bought books of old advertising and sacrificed them, cutting out the pages for his structures. Now there's a better way.

Color copiers have now progressed to the point that the copies they make look great as scale signs, especially when you weather them. So instead of cutting up those old books, find an instant-print shop that will make color copies for you for a dollar or less, then bring in those books (most likely, from a library), and copy those great old signs to your heart's content! (The same technique works well for signs photographed as color prints.)

COLOR PHOTO PRINTS FOR CHARACTERISTIC SIGNS

OK, there it is — the sign you've just got to have for that special scene or building on your layout. It could be in a book or on the side of a full-size structure, and the way to transfer it to your railroad is to shoot several photographs on color print film, have them printed, and apply a piece cut from a print to your model.

Color enlargements are expensive, but the basic prints cost less than half a buck, so shoot the sign from several distances so you'll get one close to the size you need. When the prints come back, cut out the signs, thin the edges by rubbing on fine sandpaper, color the edges with marker or paint, and glue to your building. A spray of Dullcote and a light weathering treatment will have your visitors won-

dering where you got that dandy extra-special sign!

GLOW-IN-THE-DARK NEON SIGNS

On a recent trip to a craft store I came across Tulip Neon Fabric Paint. It's sold in small plastic squeeze

bottles designed to be spread, directly from the bottle, on T-shirts or other fabric. The paint glows in the dark after it's been exposed to bright light. Several colors are available; I chose yellow, pink, and bright red.

Neon signs can be made by squeezing this paint (it has the consistency of white glue) from the applicator tip around the edges of your signs. It goes on thick and stays that way, so apply it carefully, and practice first on scrap signs. This is fun to use, especially if your layout has a day-night lighting sequence.

Tulip Neon Fabric Paint also makes great Christmas lights on buildings — just apply different colored drops around windows, doors, and roof lines.

A long waterfront pile trestle is a modeling challenge. The first tip in this chapter recommends building such a bridge upside down to ensure that the top deck comes out precisely flat.

8
Improving and detailing structures

Getting the most from some very important cast members

BUILDING DETAILED STRUCTURES is a hobby in itself, and sometimes I think it's more fun than cleaning the track or getting a balky locomotive to run well. I like building structures so much that I'll often start on a kit that I know I don't have room for on the layout. When it's done, I'll make room for it by removing a structure that's been in place for a while, or I'll put the new model on the shelf until I can find a suitable spot for it.

Because they're big models and we spend a good deal of time building them, structures are important players in the scenes we build and the stories they tell. Here are 50 tips on how to improve your structures during and after construction.

UPSIDE-DOWN BRIDGE BUILDING

Railroad bridges represent a radical departure from most structure building. The biggest difference is accuracy: Bridges have to fit, and they have to hold the track in perfect alignment for trains to run well.

This tip works equally well for kit and scratchbuilt bridges. The first step is to make a temporary bridge, usually from heavy stripwood or a chunk of lumber. Install the temporary bridge, add track, then make a tracing of the rails by placing tracing paper or thin white paper over them and rubbing with a soft lead pencil. This tracing is especially important for bridges on curves.

Now move to your workbench. Find a smooth, flat

board for a building surface, and clamp it to the bench. I use a store-bought laminated shelf with a particle-board core.

Turn your tracing of the rails over, tracing-side-down, and build the bridge floor system over it, upside down. Add the bridge ties only after the floor system is completed. This ensures that even the most complex bridge will fit your layout, and the bridge will be level. Minor inaccuracies can be compensated for by shimming the bridge abutments.

USING CARDBOARD MOCKUPS

I've learned the hard way that planning is important before embarking on a major structure-building project. But I'm no draftsman, so instead of detailed drawings, I test-build important structures for my layout by making cardboard mockups.

Just about any kind of cardboard will do, and yellow glue plus a couple of bucks' worth of 1/8" square stripwood for bracing is all you need. If you have scale drawings, photocopy them to your scale and cement them to cardboard before cutting out the walls — this gives you an even better idea of how the model will look.

Rarely does a mockup take more than a couple of

evenings to build, and it's time well spent. Working in three dimensions helps you think through how you'll construct the final model, and means you won't have a false start and wasted materials. Best of all, placing the 3-D mockup on your layout or module gives you a chance to figure out whether you like the way it looks and fits into the surrounding scene. You can make notes right on the walls and roof as you size up roof overhangs, wall heights, door placements, and so on, and you can even store trim and detail parts inside the mockup so you won't forget where they are when it comes time to build the real thing.

One word of caution: Don't make the mockups too detailed or pleasing to look at — or you're liable to leave them on the layout for years!

COLOR-SCHEME BUILDINGS

A subtle but effective way of establishing a railroady feeling on your layout is to paint lots of small structures in your road's color scheme. Prototype railroads do this, of course, and it goes a long way to reinforce their company image.

A consistent color scheme also helps weld together models that don't have consistent design or architecture. It does this so well that I've found I can achieve a satisfactory prototype company look with commercial models that are only close to correct. That means that I can have dozens of quickly built lineside sheds that look right, while spending my big chunks of time scratchbuilding only important theme structures such as stations and enginehouses.

MAKING STRUCTURES FIT BETWEEN TRACKS

To make structures like enginehouses or car shops that must fit a specific track arrangement on your layout, lay thin paper over the track and pin it in place. Trace over the rails with a soft (No. 2) lead pencil, adding notations for scenery or obstacles that the structure must accommodate.

Then take the track drawing to your workbench and build away — but it's still a good idea to check subassemblies on the layout from time to time to ensure you don't build in a hard-to-fix mistake.

A BUILDING BOARD FOR BIG STRUCTURES

I build all of my structures on some kind of portable surface that's flatter than the top of my workbench. I have a couple of old Formica-covered copying-machine platens, as well as several sheets of window glass. Their portability also means that I can leave a project on its building surface, but remove it from the bench if I start work on something more pressing.

From time to time I launch into a really big structure, something too big for my standard boards. Faced with such a big job, I bought a ready-made shelf at a hardware store. This came covered on both sides with Formica, and although it wasn't perfectly flat, I found that by placing it on the workbench

material. Simply go over the back of the printed lines with a soft No. 1 or No. 2 lead pencil, hold the template against your stock, and trace over the lines. The tracing won't be perfect, but you can clean up the lines, make the cuts, then compare each part to the printed template to refine it.

GRAPH PAPER FOR LAYERED DOWNTOWN BUILDINGS

Thanks to a lot of terrific commercial building kits, more of us are modeling downtown scenes than ever before. Multi-story downtown buildings are built up layer by layer, espe-

humped-side up, then drawing it down with a C-clamp, I could achieve the flat building surface needed for building this long high bridge.

THINNING STRIPWOOD PARTS

Occasionally you'll need stripwood of a thickness that isn't available, and nothing else will do. I choose the closest next-larger size, then make a thickness-sanding fixture to uniformly bring the dimension down to what I need.

Delrin is tough, and makes excellent depth stops for the sanding fixture. I make mine using scrap ties from Delrin flex track. Line up two or more ties on a block of scrap wood so they corral the strip being sanded, but present a broad surface that keeps you from sanding below the desired thickness. I've used this technique to make dozens of special-thickness bridge ties, and it yields accurate and repeatable results.

START A MODEL, START A LIST

The most stimulating phase of most modeling projects is the beginning, before you get bogged down with problems to solve. (Maybe that's why I start a lot more projects than I finish?) You'll always come up with great ideas as you get started, and it's important to write them down.

When I start a project I start a list, sometimes on the back of the kit instruction sheet. I jot down details to add, features to change, and things that will make the structure come to life. I don't always follow through on every idea, but at least I don't forget the best ones.

TRANSFERRING TEMPLATES

Often you need a quick and easy way to transfer an exact-size template to sheet styrene or other cially when you want to, say, make a four-story building from parts from two-story kits. Stacking stories raises the possibility of cumulative assembly errors creeping in — and maybe an unsightly leaning front.

One way to minimize such errors is to assemble the building front over graph paper, which provides lots of alignment reference to keep the wall straight and square. Tape graph paper to a flat working surface, and add a sheet of waxed paper over it. Then just keep checking the alignment of the parts against the graph lines throughout construction.

LESS-STICKY STICKY TAPE

A lot of kit instructions call for using double-sided tape (such as Scotch No. 136) to hold wood parts over full-size assembly templates. This works great, and a roll of the tape is a handy addition to your bag of modeling tricks.

Often the tape holds too well, and you'll wind up tearing away wood fibers when you remove completed assemblies from the template. The solution is to dust a little talcum powder over the exposed adhesive before positioning the wood parts. (Smells good, too!)

WARPED CAST-PLASTIC WALLS

Structures made from cast urethane or similar casting plastics sometimes include walls warped in manufacturing or packaging. An easy way to correct them is to make several light razor saw cuts about halfway into the backs of the wall (or roof) until you can gently bend it straight. Fill the slots with super glue, hold the wall straight, then hit the glue with an accelerator spray and you're ready for assembly.

STICKY CAST-PLASTIC CASTINGS

Occasionally you'll encounter an objectionable tacky surface on plastic parts made from polyester or other liquid casting plastic. Painting with Floquil Railroad Colors will usually seal the surface and give you a hard, dry surface, but to cure the problem before assembly, scrub the parts with soap and a mild abrasive.

Vigorous scrubbing with a toothbrush or fingernail brush and tooth powder, abrasive toothpaste, or my favorite, Lava soap, should do the trick. This also cleans up the castings in preparation for painting. Don't laugh, it works!

LOTS OF GLUE — WHERE YOU WON'T SEE IT

The conventional wisdom with glue has always been to use the minimum amount possible for a sound joint, but I disagree, especially on wood or paper models. Wherever a glued joint won't be seen — say, inside a building where wall or roof parts meet — I believe in building up a hefty fillet of yellow

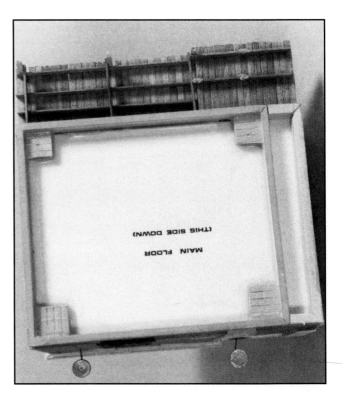

glue or 5-minute epoxy for strength and support.

The proof of the pudding came when I had "The great basement thunderstorm" several years back. A cold-water pipe in the ceiling over my layout broke, dousing the layout and a dozen wood structures with water for about half an hour. It made a mess, but because the structures had plenty of interior bracing and lots of glue, they held up nicely — even a 25-year-old Alexander Haunted House that I built in my high school days!

WHITE GLUE FOR PLASTIC BUILDING FLOORS

When you're building a plastic structure that includes a floor or base, consider attaching it with white glue. That way, should you decide to add lighting or interior detail later, you can pop the floor loose without fuss or damage.

THINNING OVERSIZE PLASTIC PARTS

Sometimes you'll find nicely made details in a plastic kit, but they'll be grossly oversize. I usually prefer to leave a gross part off a model, but occasionally you can thin a part and use it.

Here's what I did with a nice — but thick — plastic fire escape on a Heljan HO building. The rungs and uprights were too heavy, so I thinned them by sliding the moldings across the face of a medium-cut mill file. This removed about 30 percent of the thickness of the parts, leaving lots of curly plastic swarf between the rungs. To remove this I briefly dipped each part in liquid plastic cement to eat away the threads of plastic.

After allowing the cement-dipped parts to dry overnight, I painted them flat black, but didn't dry-brush them with a lighter color. Remember, dry-brushing makes things show up better, so leaving oversize parts a dead flat black or other dark color helps make them look thinner, too.

COLORING PLASTIC
BRICK WITH CHALK

Bright red brick on plastic structures can be colored and toned down quickly by rubbing the walls with plain white blackboard chalk. This also brings out the mortar line detail. Apply the chalk heavily, lightly brush away most of the loose powder, then spray on a heavy coat of Testor Dullcote to seal the chalk in place.

This isn't a technique you'll want to use on every one of your downtown structures, but it's quick and easy, and gives you an effect that looks different from coloring the mortar with paint.

SEALING POWDERY
PLASTER CASTINGS

It doesn't happen often, but you may find yourself with plaster walls (either homemade or kit) that are powdery or chalky. To save them, apply a heavy, soaking coat of full-strength Floquil Crystal Cote,

Floquil Glaze, or Krylon Clear Flat Fixative spray as a binder. Allow the binder to dry for a week if possible, then proceed with assembly and painting.

BUFFING METAL CASTINGS
WITH A SUEDE BRUSH

When you clean up white metal castings, try polishing them with a brass-bristled suede brush after removing flash with knife and files. The brass bristles knock off tool marks and fine parting lines and remove oxidation. Paint will adhere better to the castings, and they'll look better, too.

INSTALLING CASTINGS TEMPORARILY

Sometimes you'll want to have window, door, and trim castings in place for painting, weathering, and blending with the surrounding siding, but you need to remove them later for glazing. You can use small dabs of white or yellow glue for this, but a better way is to attach the castings with small dabs of mortician's wax.

Mortician's wax is used for theatrical makeup, and it's just sticky enough for this purpose (dollhouse miniatures hobbyists use a similar product call Mini-Hold). Be sure to key the castings for replacement in their respective openings.

TOOTHPICK HANDLES FOR PAINTING

To make a quick-and-dirty painting handle for a part with no back or hidden side, find (or drill) a hole in its back surface, then glue in a round toothpick. This is perfect for chimneys and for wheels on cars and trucks.

CONCRETE PLATFORMS
AND SIDEWALKS

Sheet styrene makes excellent concrete sidewalks and station platforms (Evergreen Scale Models offers sheet stock already scribed with sidewalk-size squares). The trick to achieving realism is to introduce some irregularities into the surface.

Try making a sidewalk or loading platform from individual styrene slabs, adding thin paper shims

under a few to vary the height and make some (not all) of the slabs tilted. Use the back of an X-acto blade to carve in cracks and pits. Finally, vary the look here and there by piecing together a few concrete areas with sections of the cast-plastic platforms that come with kit structures.

RECYCLING OLD ROLLING STOCK

Railroads often convert old cars to lineside structures, and you can too. Remove trucks, couplers, and safety appliances, block up the car, and paint it

appropriately for its new role. Don't get carried away, though: Just because you have 20 out-of-service boxcars doesn't mean your layout can use 20 lineside storage sheds made from them!

GETTING STRUCTURES TO SIT LEVEL

The free-flowing scenery on *Model Railroader's* Pennsylvania project layout posed quite a challenge when it came time to place the structures. My biggest problem was getting them to sit level.

The best solution was to cut a piece of 1" thick Styrofoam bead board about 2" wider and longer than the footprint of the structure. I placed this on the scenery and drew a line around it. With a mat

knife I cut the scenery base so I could either push it down or remove it.

I squeezed a bead of white glue around the edge of the bead board and pushed it into the hole. Using a small line level I wiggled the bead board until it was level in both directions. After the glue dried I spread Sculptamold to blend the bead board into the scenery. Setting structures on the level spot was then easy.

PINNING DOWN YOUR STRUCTURES

As time goes on I've learned that it makes more and more sense to make structures removable from the layout or diorama by pinning them instead of gluing. This is surprisingly little work, and it's a great convenience to be able to lift the model off for

cleaning or repair. This is almost mandatory in cases where you know you'll have to work on things behind the structure, and it's a great way to make fences less breakable.

The simplest pin is the dulled point from a safety pin; you can also use a piece of $1/32$" wire. One pin is enough for some structures, but I usually add two, on opposite corners. Drill into the corner bracing and cement each pin in place with super glue or epoxy.

Position the structure on the layout and press down to mark the locations for holes, then drill. Test-fit, then cover the bottom of the structure with Saran Wrap so you can work scenic texture close to the foundation without gluing the building to the layout. If you have a hard time finding the holes, add tiny spots of bright color to each one. They'll be hidden by the structure.

SIMPLE CARDBOARD FOUNDATIONS

Many structure kits don't include a foundation, but you'll want to add something to raise the building up out of the scenery and ground cover. Cut a simple slab of heavy cardboard (a piece of leftover mat board from a picture framing shop is perfect, and usually yours for the asking) so it will sit flush with the edges of the walls, then glue in place. Paint the edges — the only part you'll see — with Polly S

Concrete paint. Don't waste time with a fancy treatment here: After all, most of the foundation will be buried in ground cover.

HEAVY FOUNDATIONS FROM STONE RETAINING WALLS

To model heavy cut-stone foundations, cut sections from plastic or plaster retaining walls or tun-

nel portals. Relatively few structures had such underpinnings, but the big stones make a welcome relief from the more common concrete foundations, and they're easy to make.

SHINGLE ROOFS WHERE YOU DON'T EXPECT THEM

Plastic buildings usually have excellent siding and trim details, but some of them fall short on the roof, which is, after all, the part we see most of the time. Try substituting a Campbell shingle roof on some of your plastic buildings. You'll be surprised how far this goes toward making a plastic shed look like a model built from a craftsman-style kit.

EXTRA HANDS FOR GLUING ON THE ROOF

I never seem to have enough hands when it comes time to add the roof to a structure, especially when the glue will take a while to set. A couple of strips of 2"-wide masking tape and some metal weights make a good aid to hold the roof down, and it frees me up to check all sides of the building for a proper fit. For some structures a plastic sandwich bag filled with sand works as well or better.

SOOT STREAKS FROM CHIMNEYS

One of the easiest ways to suggest that there's

something going on inside a model structure is to streak soot down the roof from a stovepipe or chimney.

You can accomplish the task any number of ways, but my favorite is to wet the roofing below the chimney or pipe with solvent, then gently stroke an almost-dry brush with a touch of black paint down the roofing material. Don't ever get the black above the chimney — gravity wouldn't take it there — and don't dry-brush a lighter color over the soot.

FILLING ROOF CRACKS WITH TAR

Whether you have real gaps or not, full-strength Mars Black acrylic tube color makes good tar to

represent seams in flat roofs. Apply the paint with a fine brush, or use a glue syringe to build up a little relief by applying a heavier bead. This also works well to caulk the joints where the walls of masonry buildings meet the roof at right angles.

ROOF CHARACTER FOR FREE

It takes only seconds during construction to add a subtle swayback to the ridgepole of a structure, and the result is a welcome relief from the perfectly straight roofline. Just carve, sand, or file a gentle curve into the ridgepole piece, deepest at the center

and tapering toward the ends. You may need to preform the roof sections with your fingers to make them conform to the shape.

This is a great way to incorporate a little rundown flavor in a few of your structures, but keep it subtle. And remember that character can easily become caricature: Unless you're modeling a cartoon line like the Toonerville Trolley or the Fiddletown & Copperopolis, use this trick only on one or two buildings in a larger scene.

MODERN MEMBRANE ROOFING

If your layout operates in the here and now you can achieve a different look or improve an ugly plastic roof by modeling a membrane roof covering. There are different kinds, but this type of replacement roof is installed by covering the old roofing with a rubberlike sheet.

I modeled a membrane roof by covering the kit texture with facial tissue held in place with super glue. Position the tissue, soak through with the glue, then trim. Paint the membrane white with a touch of silver, then dry-brush heavily. It's OK if some of the underlying texture shows through.

TARPAPER ROOFING OVER PLASTIC

We have dozens upon dozens of European-proto-

type structure kits in HO scale, and usually it takes only a change here and there to Americanize them. Often the roof is the hardest feature to change, but here's a tip you can use to literally paper over toofancy roofing.

Cut a heavy institutional paper towel into scale 30"-wide strips, then apply them as tarpaper over the kit roof. Super glue is best for this, but I've also used full-strength matte medium. Work the wet toweling into the original roof texture with your fingernail so traces of it will show through later.

Paint the toweling to represent tarpaper, then dry-brush.

REAL COPPER FLASHING

Stained glass hobbyists use $\frac{1}{4}$"-wide strips of

copper foil with self-adhesive backing to wrap glass sections so they can be soldered together. This material is great for modeling copper flashing on the roofs of buildings, especially those with slate roofs.

To use, cut a piece of copper foil to the general length needed, lay it on a flat surface, and slice it to the correct width. Place the strip on the roof for a trial fit, then remove the paper backing to expose the stickum and lay the strip in place.

Smooth the copper down with your fingernail. To form a straight ridge line, smooth the foil over a length of wire on the ridge of the structure. The foil strips can be painted a weathered green color, or treated with A-West Patina-It, a pickling solution for copper.

EASY DIAMOND-PATTERN SHINGLES

A different-looking, diamond-shaped asphalt or slate shingle roof can be modeled using pinking shears. Dressmakers use pinking shears for cutting

out fabric over a paper pattern. Although not cheap, a good pair will last a lifetime, and can be used to model diamond-shaped asphalt shingles on hundreds of structures. You can buy a pair in most fabric shops. Look for the ones with the smallest teeth.

I draw parallel lines on bond paper, then cut strips following the lines. Glue the strips to the roof

so that the points of the diamond are staggered (see photo). After the roof is complete, paint slate shingles with Polly S Reefer Gray to which you've added a little green. Weather with a black wash and dry-brush with white.

ASPHALT SHINGLES

Modern asphalt shingles are seldom modeled because of the lack of good looking miniature shingles in a variety of scales and colors. Until recently only Campbell rolled wood shake-shingles and strips of black paper were readily available.

Now, with the widespread use of laser cutting, several manufacturers offer accurate asphalt

shingles laser cut from colored sheets of crack and peel adhesive-backed paper. To use, just remove a strip of shingles from the package, peel off the paper backing, and press into place. They can be used as is for a new structure or painted. If you have enough buildings with asphalt shingles you can really change the look and era of your layout.

Laser-cut shingles are available in many different styles and interesting colors, including green, pink, beige, and light blue. The ones I use are from Precision Lasercraft (see Addresses).

MODELING A BADLY DEFORMED BUILDING

It isn't a trick you want to use over and over again on your railroad, but a crooked or twisted building can be a real eye-catcher on a layout or diorama. The reason is that we're all used to seeing 90-degree angles and plumb walls, and when we encounter a structure where those rules don't pertain, it immediately signals that something's wrong: The building has settled, aged, or otherwise become a victim of time. (See page 58, bottom photo.)

The bad news is that modeling a building that's out of whack is actually more effort than one that's square. All those twists and turns mean that things won't line up properly at the corners, so you'll have to do considerable planning on the drawing board or with 3-D mockups before you start producing the model itself. Trust me — it's worth it!

BACKDATING STRUCTURES

You can't turn a ranch house into a Victorian mansion, but occasionally it's possible to backdate a building by altering doors, windows, and trim details.

Older brick buildings have arched windows and

doors (the arch was the only way to make the top of the opening until steel lintels came along), and generally speaking, older buildings have smaller windows with more panes. The photo shows a garage from an HO Revell suburban house backdated by changing the 1950s-style tilt-up door to the more traditional hinged arrangement.

BUILD IT BACKWARDS IF YOU CAN

Kits look great, but if you follow the instructions exactly, the building will look the same as dozens or even hundred of others. One way around this is to evaluate each kit to see if the walls could be rearranged to build the model backwards — a mirror image of the original design.

Sometimes this won't be possible, and you'll have to find some other way to make your model distinctive. To make sure you won't run into trouble because of your redesign, photocopy the plans or the walls and cut out the parts, then test-assemble them in the new configuration you have in mind.

DETAILING BUILDING ROOFS

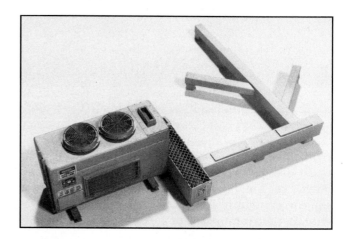

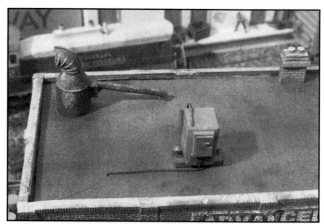

The first thing visitors notice as they look down on your layout is the roofs of your structures. If your roofs are detailed they'll think the whole layout is superdetailed, whether it is or not. That's right! If

you detail the roofs the rest of the layout will look more interesting by implication.

My friend Pete Laier puts all kinds of neat-looking stuff on his roofs. The best-looking details are made from a wide selection of modern diesel detailing parts, particularly fans, grills and gratings. Pete adds these to an assortment of styrene boxes made from Evergreen styrene, adds bits of wire, and finishes the detail with other scrapbox items. The easiest to build are industrial air conditioning units with spiderlike ductwork spread over the roof.

PAINTING CAST-METAL BUILDINGS

It's a real chore to paint those small cast metal structures made by Woodland Scenics and S.S. Ltd. These buildings have doors, windows, trim, and details cast into the walls, and I've found that no matter how hard I try, I can't paint a crisp outline around these details. The best excuse I've found for my unsteady hand is that the castings have lost their crisp, sharp edges. This is due, in part, because of the way the castings are made to release from the mold, and because the molds wear down during the production runs.

To get around all these problems I first prime the castings with gray automotive primer. I let it dry long enough so I can't smell the thinner. (Drying can be speeded up by leaving the castings in a warm oven — not over 170° F. — overnight.) Next, I dab paint into the most recessed parts of the castings — this can be the walls between the windows, the interior, or the surface of the roof. Sometimes I'll use both water-based and solvent-based paints on the same structure.

After the base coat dries I carefully paint the raised portions of the castings with a contrasting color — the doors and their frames, the windows, trim, and undersides of the roof and the gutters. Then I color details like the chimney, foundation, and roof braces, and complete any touch-up to correct where the trim color may have overlapped the base color.

To blend the paint together and give the illusion that it was carefully painted I flow on a wash made from 1/2 teaspoon of lampblack (called lampblack in oil, sold in large art and hardware stores) dissolved in a pint of mineral spirits (paint thinner). I lay the building sides flat on the workbench. With a large, soft brush, I apply a brushful of the wash and let it flow into the casting surface. The wash will outline all the raised detail and settle into the lowest parts of the casting. Sometimes with clapboard structures I'll raise the bottom of the casting slightly so the wash settles up under the clapboards, providing a shadow effect. When the wash dries, lightly dry-brush the very tops of the castings with white to

bring out all the excellent cast-in detail.

Painting mistakes tend to disappear after the black wash, and become really invisible after the dry-brushing.

DETAILS TO OMIT

This is a book on detailing, but it's as important to

know what details you can omit as it is to understand what needs to be included. This is particularly the case when you've build a structure without knowing exactly where it will go on the railroad, and when it comes time to install it, you realize that two or three sides won't be visible.

Take a minute or two to strip details off the invisible sides so they can be placed where they will be seen, even if it's with another building or in another scene altogether. It's work enough to detail the parts of your railroad that visitors can see and appreciate, and you should never spend a minute on what won't be appreciated. (When you're building a structure for a specific, known, slot on your layout, give some thought to omitting window and door details, even paint, on the sides that won't ever be seen.)

BENDING BUILDINGS

Planning a layout or a scene from a catalog is all la-dee-dah compared to the real-life practice of shoe-horning buildings into the space left available between the tracks. One idea that can really help you is the thought of "bending" buildings: It's not that

hard to make rectangles or squares into parallelograms or even irregular shapes.

One rule to remember is that as long as the "face" of your structure looks at the viewer the sides and rear can be oriented about any old way and no one will be the wiser — overall, the scene will still be convincing.

STYRENE AND PLIOBOND DON'T MIX!

For 30 years I've been using Pliobond, a flexible, rubberlike adhesive, for a couple of applications. One is where you need its contact-cementing characteristics (coat each material separately, then join, without glue oozing out or going everywhere); the other is for installing clear window glazing, where its characteristic of staying where you put it (not running) keeps it off the "glass" surface.

But I've also discovered a key incompatibility: Pliobond reacts with sheet styrene. It doesn't seem to affect molded styrene much, and you can still use it to install glazing, but coating large sheet-styrene surfaces with Pliobond to, say, install corrugated siding or roofing texture will eventually lead to warping and disaster. I've had to replace one large roof entirely (it warped in spite of extensive bracing), and a structure with corrugated material glued to the sides also warped badly over a period of about 8 years.

It seems like solvents from the Pliobond slowly seep into the styrene, soften it, and allow other forces (gravity, twisting) to have their way. The older the structure, the more distorted it becomes. I still use Pliobond, sometimes thinned with MEK or Testor Liquid Plastic Cement, but not on structures that will include large sheet styrene parts!

PROPS FOR TIPPY BUILDINGS

Ever built a tippy building? That's one where, after you've assembled the walls, the model is next to impossible to handle at the workbench. Maybe it's

configured to fit into a hillside, split-level style, or maybe there's some heavy part in one corner that makes the model flop over on its side.

I usually spend a couple of frustrating hours propping the model up with blocks or scrap lumber so I can work on it before I remember to glue in one or two simple props made of kit runner (sprue), dowel, or some other scrap material to keep the model on an even keel. When work is complete, I clip or saw away the props, then install the building on the layout where it won't ever tip over again.

TRY A DIFFERENT DOOR

I didn't remember to take a photo of this Mainline & Siding Structure Co. truck repair shed before I modified it, but imagine how it would look with a shop door only about two-thirds the size of the one shown here. Something bothered me about the model all during construction, but it wasn't until it was completed that I figured it out: The main door, which should have been tall enough to accommodate a truck, was just too small for the building to look right.

Once I had the problem diagnosed, it took only a few minutes to pop out the kit-supplied casting, find a larger, more-appropriate Grandt Line plastic door, paint, and install.

The moral of the story: Just because it comes in the kit doesn't mean it's the best door, window, or other detail part to make a pleasing model. You should be skeptical — and replacing a few parts may mean you'll like the finished model a lot more!

A QUICK STATION PLATFORM

One evening I was rummaging through my materials bin looking for something to use for a station platform. The platform would be about 24" back from the front edge of the layout, so I didn't have to come up with the ultimate in detail; in fact, I was looking for something that would do the job quickly.

I ran across a package of Heki-dur building material, made by the Heki Co. of Germany (see Addresses). This is a lightweight expanded foam about $1/16$" thick; the top surface has a texture molded in, and comes painted in $5^3/_4$" x $11^3/_4$" sheets.

I chose material No. 7013, Sidewalk, which has slightly overscale sidewalk panels and came painted gray. It took only a couple of swipes with a hobby knife, a couple of $\frac{1}{16}$"-square bits of stripwood to make a curb, and some yellow carpenter's glue to make my platform. When cut, the raw edge of the foam material even looks like concrete texture. Heki-dur also comes in random stone, cut stone, and a couple of brick patterns.

AN EASY-TO-MAKE TIN ROOF

I was building a filler structure — one of those semi-anonymous little structures that fills out a scene without calling much attention to itself — and I decided I wanted a slightly different roof texture. A simple raised-seam tin roof came to mind.

The roof base material forms most of the sheathing as well. I cut .030" styrene sheet to size for the three roof panels and glued them into place on the walls. The raised ribs are Evergreen HO 2x4 styrene strip, a bit larger than scale, but the right size to show up.

Painting was even easier. I gave the roof a brush coat of Polly S Reefer Gray, and followed immedi-

ately with light streaks of Polly S Rust. I allowed this to dry, then applied my standard Black Wash (Chapter 1), followed by some streaks of Rustall Rust solution.

After the paints and washes dried overnight, I blended the rusty colors together with a light dusting of rust-colored pastel chalks, applied with a brush.

REVIVING AN OLD STRUCTURE

While rummaging through a box of old structures I found a building I'd forgotten about. It was a small false-front western general store. I remembered spending a lot of time building it. With a little modification it would be the perfect centerpiece for a small diorama I was planning.

The first job was to clean the building. Even though it was in a sealed box it was filthy. I cleaned the roof by giving it a good scrubbing with a wet brush. Then, after cleaning the brush in warm soapy water, I brushed down the walls and porch.

The original front porch and roof had broken off in storage. I reattached them with a few drops of super glue. I also added a brick chimney to the rear roof. This was glued slightly askew to look like it was about to fall off.

After the structure dried I started repainting. I gave the whole building a light coating of Basic Black Wash (the formula is in Chapter 1) to darken and unify the coloring. Next I added window shades made from small squares of cardboard inside the window over the glazing. I painted out several of the small windows with gloss black paint. Turning the structure over, I dry-brushed all raised surfaces with Polly S Reefer White.

. . . AND GOING FROM WEST TO EAST

At this point I had to decide what the structure would be used for. I had a neat-looking lobster sign made from the end of a swizzle stick and a piece of plastic sign salvaged from an old kit. I fitted the sign to the front of the building and glued it in place. Instantly the structure became a lobster pound. I made a small sign on my laser printer that said "Dave's Fish & Chips."

Next I prepared the diorama base, a small rectangle of 2"-thick Styrofoam. I shaved the sides so they sloped away from the center, helping to lead the viewer's eye to the structure. The structure was set in place and rotated until the best angle was found. I drew a pencil line to outline the base.

I hollowed out the Styrofoam under one rear corner of the building. In this spot I planned to build a corner of the brick foundation, just enough to show that the building has a foundation. (The easiest way to turn a western structure into one that's at home

in other — colder — parts of the country is to put a foundation under it. I've modified many Colorado storefronts into eastern waterfront shanties with only the addition of a brick foundation and some nautical detail.)

After the foundation was built, colored, and installed, I set the structure in place. It aligned with the foundation and looked okay, so I applied a thin bead of glue to the structure base, set it on the pencil outline, and held it flat with weights on the roof. I let the glue dry overnight, then started the scenery.

I added a dirt road made from a piece of 1/8" Fome-

cor board. I used Sculptamold to mate the edges of the road with the surrounding scenery. The surface of the road was painted with earth-colored latex paint. While the paint was wet I sprinkled on fine dirt. Next I glued on several layers of scenic foam grass, and finished with a heavy application of static grass. A dead tree, logs, barrels, fences and other details were added, all to emphasize and complement the building.

To finish the diorama I added lots of pre-painted and weathered detail castings, and the symbol of the New England waterfront, a pile of old lobster traps.

Dave's Fish & Chips started out as a kit-built boomtown western store. Almost 10 years and a major facelift later, it's been transformed into a Down East lobster pound, with details and scenic treatment providing the keys to this minor player's new role.

Spend a little time at trackside, and you'll come away convinced that railroading is a dirty business. Grease and oil stains are typical of a working line, and they cost next to nothing to add to your layout.

9

Weathering and airbrushing

Mastering simple painting techniques to enhance your modeling

FOUR FACTORS INFLUENCE HOW we see our models and the scenes we build for them: form, color, texture, and pattern. Of these, color is the one we can exercise the most control over most often, in fact, we can change the color of any item on our layout just by painting it.

Over the years I've convinced myself that painting is the most important step in every modeling project, because when the project is completed, what I and my viewers will see is paint. Many moons ago I purchased my first airbrush and taught myself to use it by trial and error (a lot of error!). Since then, I've settled on the airbrush as the best way to paint just about any model I build.

MODELING DIESEL CRUD

The ground around diesel facilities is sopped with oil and grime. To make realistic diesel crud mix one part silver paint with two parts black and enough water (or thinner) to double the volume. Mix well.

Daub this mixture liberally around your servicing facility. Don't be fussy — drip it on the track, puddle it on the service stand, spread it on the ground and on all the ballast in the area. Trail it down the middle of the track near the servicing facility.

GREASE STAINS IN A BOTTLE

A railroad's main line and yards are in many respects grease trails, and there's usually at least a trace of oil between the rails, especially where trains stand for long periods or where slow drags struggle up a grade. I keep a small bottle of thinned Polly S Grimy Black with my scenery materials specifically for adding stains to track and roads.

The stains are easy to apply, especially when the

track ballast or road surface is still damp with bonding spray or paint. Dip the tip of a small brush into the thinned paint, then lightly touch it where grease or oil would be. It will disperse realistically into the ballast, and stain roads nicely, too.

WEATHERING BRIDGES AND GIRDERS

Recently I built a model of a steel girder bridge using parts from several plastic kits plus an assortment of styrene strips and sheets. When I finished the bridge was a patchwork of colors. To paint it I relied on my old standby, Floquil Railroad Colors in spray cans.

I set the bridge upside down on a large sheet of newspaper and coated all surfaces with Floquil Primer. When dry enough to touch I turned the bridge over and finished priming. I let the bridge dry for several days, then I applied a light spray of flat Weathered Black, just

a fine mist. I hung the bridge on a bent piece of coat hanger wire and let it dry for a week.

I weathered the bridge with a thin wash of Floquil Weathered Black, alternating with a thin wash of 50-50 Rail Brown and Roof Brown to make corroded areas. Both washes were applied with a large brush while tipping the bridge so the wash ran into all the nooks and crannies. I gave the girders and panels an overall rust wash using Rustall.

After the bridge had several days to dry I drybrushed it lightly with Polly S white to bring out rivet heads and girder edges.

WEATHERING WITH DRY PIGMENTS

Most modelers have tried weathering models with powdered pastel-colored chalks. An alternative weathering medium is dry pigments. Their intended use is to color dry cement or plaster, and they won't change the chemical reaction or setting times. The pigments are made by grinding rock and earth into a powder-like texture similar to face powder. Pigments are available in realistic earth colors and are sold under the trade names Driad,

Color-Rite, and Empire.

They can be found in hardware, paint, and hobby stores, and through the Walthers catalog. Do not confuse dry pigment colors with dry tempera paint; the latter won't work for weathering models.

A BASIC OLD RUST COLOR

Real rust comes in many shades, and while fresh rust is indeed bright orange, usually rust is both redder and browner. Both Floquil and Polly S Rust are too orange for my tastes, so I mix my own "old rust" by combining three parts Rust with one part Roof Brown.

RUSTALL WEATHERING TREATMENT

I'm willing to try just about anything in the quest for realism, so I bought a Rustall weathering kit as soon as the product appeared on the scene. The kit consists of four bottles: a medium-red rust wash, a thin black wash, a fine gray powder, and a water-soluble flat finish. Following the instructions with the kit will yield excellent results.

I seem to use the rust solution most, and fortu-

nately it's available separately. I prefer Testor Dullcote to the clear flat, and my standard India ink in rubbing alcohol is a good subtitute for the black, but the basic technique of color over color is a dandy. The source is Kuras Design Group (see Addresses).

DRY-BRUSHING WITH ACRYLICS

If I've said it once I've said it hundreds of times: "dry-brush everything." Structures, especially, benefit from dry-brushing to tie all their separate elements and colors together.

I've always favored a stiff, short-bristled brush for dry-brushing solvent-based paints like Floquil Railroad Colors. Nowadays, with water-based acrylic and latex paints taking over, I recommend using a soft, camel- or squirrel-hair brush. The soft bristles absorb some water from the paint and hold the moisture and color longer than stiff bristles can.

DRY-BRUSHING VS. PARTING LINES

Dry-brushing is a great way to bring out molded-in detail, but the technique can also bring out flaws and detail that shouldn't be there. Good examples are mold-parting lines, where the mold halves meet on plastic or metal parts; or ejector-pin marks, the little round depressions where the pins that push plastic parts out of the molds meet the mold surface. Dry-brushing will gloriously highlight these unprototypical manufacturing artifacts, and we don't want that.

Eliminating parting lines on plastic parts is fairly easy: Where possible, draw a hobby knife blade

along the line to adze, or scrape, the line away, then daub on some MEK (solvent plastic cement) with a brush to blend the surface texture. Filing the lines and brushing with a suede brush is the best treatment for larger white metal parts; raised ejector-pin marks can be carefully shaved off flat surfaces, and depressed ones are best filled with a drop of thick super glue and sanded flush.

SCALE EFFECT FOR YOUR COLORS

Military modelers use a concept called scale effect to adjust colors for viewing distance. Colors lighten perceptibly and become muted as you move away from any object, meaning that a prototype color chip is inaccurate for scale models, because we're always looking at them from the equivalent of 60 or more feet away.

So lighten all your colors, and lighten them more for buildings or other items that will always be at a considerable distance from the viewer. This principle is why those boxcars or diesels painted with the paint made from the color chip that the real railroad used look too dark. One good guide for choosing colors is to use color photo prints of the real thing, mixing your colors to match the print. You'll be surprised how light the colors will be. Choose a compromise that you're comfortable with, and err on the light side for scenery colors and structures, and on the dark side for your trains. This will help the trains pop out of their surroundings.

WEATHERING OVER WEATHERING

If you like the initial weathering treatment on the model, try repeating it . Simply go through the basic steps of wash, followed by pastels, followed by a light dry-brushing all over again. The net effect will be to build the illusion of depth, just as with the initial weathering treatment.

I suggest experimenting with this double weathering technique before trying it on your favorite model — but that's good advice for any technique that you're trying for the first time.

APPLE BARREL PAINTS

If you're looking to try another hobby paint, one that's perfect for painting and weathering structures, then get yourself a set of Apple Barrel craft paints. These paints are not new; they've been used by professional model builders for years. About a dozen colors are available in 5-ounce plastic squeeze bottles. These paints are water-based acrylics and sold in most large craft stores.

They work best when brushed over a primed surface. The manufacturer recommends two coats with about one hour drying time between applications, but I've had good coverage with just one coat

over wood and plaster. Metal and plastic models must be primed. I use either Floquil's Gray Primer or cheap gray automotive primer, both in spray cans.

Apple Barrel paints can be thinned with water to make weathering washes. They're also great for dry-brushing.

WATERCOLORS FOR WEATHERING STRUCTURES

A good way to get your feet wet and try weathering models is with tube watercolors. Their biggest advantage is that the colors are easy to mix and apply. Spread a little of each color on a flat sheet of glass or plastic, dilute with water, and apply with a brush, sprayer, or swab. If you don't like the results,

just wash the weathering off the model with a clean, damp cotton swab, or by spraying with more water.

Tube watercolors are available in craft, art and some hobby shops in sets or individually. I recommend buying separate colors: Start with black, white, medium green, burnt umber, raw sienna and red. Almost all the weathering shades you'll need can be mixed from this selection.

The best use on structures is to make soot streaks around chimneys, rust running from nut-bolt-washer castings, green moss on the north side of a stone foundation, and colorful mortar on brick siding.

CHOOSING YOUR FIRST AIRBRUSH

A lot of what you read about airbrushes is written for artists, who typically spray very thin paints and dyes onto paper. This is a whole different ball game from spraying our heavy pigmented modeling paints, so it's no small wonder that a lot of modelers have trouble with this tool.

At last count I owned seven airbrushes, including a couple of fancy double-action jobs where you can control both the air volume and the amount of paint with the finger button. But over the years I've come to the conclusion that the simple ones work best for me. For years I used a Binks Wren B, and the one that's hooked up to my compressor and hanging next

to the paint booth now is an inexpensive Paasche H with a No. 3 — or medium — tip.

If you're disappointed that I'm using these relatively crude instruments, I'll add that because these simple airbrushes are external-mix (they don't have an internal needle valve, so the paint never gets inside the airbrush body), they're easy to clean, which is a big factor in getting me to use the airbrush often. Also, simple airbrushes have less to go wrong, and they're easier to rebuild when worn or damaged.

COMPRESSOR RECOMMENDATIONS

If you're going to paint with an airbrush, you need an air compressor to go with it — period. I've tried using canned propellants and refillable air tanks, but nothing beats the convenience or long-term economy of an electric compressor.

There are several choices. For years I used a basic Binks diaphragm compressor, which was relatively quiet but suffered from pulsation in the air pressure at the airbrush. A 12-foot hose from the compressor to the brush helped this, and the problem was solved when I added a cheap refillable air tank between the compressor and regulator. The tank served both as a surge supressor and an efficient moisture separator.

About 5 years ago I bought a Campbell-Hausfield 3/4-h.p. tank-mounted compressor, and I quickly realized that this is the way to go. The rig includes a pressure gauge and regulator, and shuts down when the tank is charged up. It even has wheels and a handle, so it's easy to move around. In fact, its only disadvantage is that it makes enough noise to raise the dead.

If noise is a major consideration for you, look into the noiseless compressors available from art-supply houses. Similar to the silent compressors used in refrigerators, they are truly close to noiseless — but they'll set you back several hundred dollars. They may well be worth it for apartment dwellers, or if you work far into the night while the rest of the family sleeps.

THE RIGHT PRESSURE SETTING FOR AIRBRUSHING

Several variables come into play in selecting the right air pressure for spraying with your airbrush. That "your airbrush" is important, and you should start your quest for the perfect pressure by reading the manufacturer's recommendations.

Most of the time I airbrush thinned Floquil Railroad Colors at 17-18 psi, and that's not a bad starting point for establishing your optimum pressure. Thin the paint you plan to use, load up the airbrush, and try various volume settings while spraying a sheet of white cardboard or an old model. Evaluate the results, then raise or lower the pressure about three pounds and test again.

The new water-base colors require an extra pound or two of pressure, but not much more than that. Your average pressure should fall somewhere between 12 and 24 psi — anything higher than 24 means something is wrong: Maybe the paint isn't thin enough, the color control isn't providing enough paint, or the needle/tip combination is too fine for the relatively heavy paints we spray on models.

USING AN ORGANIC-CARTRIDGE RESPIRATOR MASK

All of us are a lot more aware that we used to be of the dangers of solvents and chemicals, and some of the most dangerous ones we use in modeling are paints, especially when we spray them. I confess that for years I sprayed Floquil paints without much in the way of ventilation or protection, but as I learned more about the hazards I became more and more concerned.

Nowadays I've got a permanent sheet-metal spray booth with a blower that makes my hair point toward the booth, but such a rig isn't in the cards for everyone. If your ventilation (and you'd better have some!) is such that you can still smell the solvent in the paint, you can achieve a measure of protection if you wear a cartridge respirator mask with replaceable cartridges that absorb organic compounds. You can find these at large hardware stores or farm centers, and the cost is reasonable. Remember, if you can smell a solvent, it's probably not good for you — and even water-base paints contain pigments that you don't want down inside your lungs.

LATEX EXAM GLOVES FOR SPRAY PAINTING

A box of disposable latex examination gloves is an essential part of my airbrushing equipment. I buy them 100 at a time from a discount drugstore, and don at least one every time I crank up the airbrush. The glove allows me to hold a model while spraying, and it means I won't have to douse that hand with solvent or spend time scrubbing away paint residue. Be sure to specify unpowdered, non-sterile gloves: You don't want the powder on your models, and you don't want to pay the extra price for sterile gloves.

CONVENIENT AIRBRUSH BOTTLES

Typically, airbrushes come with open color cups, and with special syphon bottles that have caps threaded to fit the bottles provided with the airbrush. If you use these bottles, you'll spend way too much time cleaning them after each airbrushing session. Nuts to that.

Take the siphon-bottle cap apart and install the siphon in the cap of a kind of bottle that you have a lot of: a Floquil bottle, or a Kodak plastic 35mm film can. The film cans are disposable — I just pour out the leftover paint and discard them — and having a cap that fits Floquil bottles mean I can simply plug the siphon top into any bottle of thinned paint and go to it.

STRAINING PAINT TO BE AIRBRUSHED

You may have heard this tip before, but good advice is worth repeating: You should strain every single drop of paint you plan to shoot through an airbrush. I figured this out about 15 years ago, and since then I've had maybe two paint clogs in hundreds and hundreds of airbrushing sessions.

To pre-strain your paint, thin it per the manufacturer's instructions for airbrushing, then pour it through a fine tea strainer or artist's enamel powder strainer (used for cloisonné work), through a small funnel, and into the airbrush container. You'll be amazed how many paint clumps you'll filter out, and how big they are — even from a brand-new bottle of paint. Any one of them would have brought your spray-painting session to a screeching halt.

AIRBRUSH SIPHON STRAINERS

Better yet, a couple of airbrush makers have offered a cylindrical strainer that fits right over the siphon tube that extends down into the paint bottle. Badger had one, I think, and there was at least one other brand. They do such a good job that when you

find one, dig out your wallet and buy two of them.

YOU NEED AN AIRBRUSH HOLDER

Because most airbrushes will fall over if you set them down on a flat surface, I used to find myself standing at the paint booth juggling both a loaded airbrush and a half-painted model. This is not good, and eventually it means something will be dropped.

After repainting a couple of models and replacing the damaged color control assembly on my airbrush, I added an airbrush holder to the side of my paint booth. You can find a couple of holders at your art supply store, or you can make up something simple by bending coat hanger wire. You'll be amazed how much having a place to set the airbrush simplifies airbrushing.

A TURNTABLE FOR YOUR SPRAY BOOTH

The simplest painting aid in my shop is a plastic Rubbermaid turntable, the kind that you put in the kitchen cabinet so you can find the bottle of cinnamon when you need it. Mine cost just a couple of bucks years ago, and it must be useful because it's caked with paint from use.

CUSTOM MODEL HOLDERS

Wire coat hangers seem to breed in most closets, and nowadays cleaning establishments even have programs to recycle them. Don't take 'em all back, though, because they're handy for making simple model holders for spray painting.

You can cut and bend the hanger wire any way you want, and even add pads of masking tape to cover sharp edges and stick the model to the modified hanger. It's easy to form the wire to poke up into the interior of a plastic carbody, and it's just as easy to toss out the used hanger when the job is done.

A STANDARD ROUTINE FOR AIRBRUSHING

Airbrushing is the best way to paint models, period, and it's not a difficult skill to master if you're willing to buy the right equipment, follow directions, and spend some time practicing. Once you've achieved proficiency, it's helpful to settle on a standard routine for preparing, painting, and cleaning up afterward. Here's mine:

1. Prepare the models and parts. Cleaning the airbrush is work, and to minimize the amount of time I spend cleaning, I rarely airbrush only one model. Instead, I try to prepare parts from two or more projects for spraying at the same time. One model may be ready for a final coat of clear flat finish, another for a primer or overall color coat, and a third may have window and door or detail castings ready for painting.

Clean all the parts to be painted, dry them, and

arrange them by color on sticky-side-up masking tape on scrap cardboard. Write the color for the parts on the face of each cardboard flat, and arrange the flats near your paint booth in the order to be sprayed: clear coatings first, then light colors, dark colors, and metallics last. This sequence makes it easiest to clean the airbrush between colors, and reduces the problem of unwanted spots.

2. Prepare the paint. Next get out the paints. Strain each color into a clean container, dilute with thinner, and add 5 percent Floquil Glaze to Floquil colors. Arrange the prepared colors like the flats of parts, from clear to light to dark, placing the thinned paints right next to the cardboard flats.

3. PAINT! Crank up your compressor, adjust the pressure, and test the first color on a scrap model or piece of white cardboard. When you have a good smooth spray pattern, paint the first flat of parts. Run a little thinner through the airbrush between colors, change bottles, and paint each successive color and flat of parts. Even after years of sticking to this routine I'm always amazed that applying the paint takes so little time compared to getting ready and cleaning up.

4. Clean up. Remove the painted parts and paints from the spraying area, then thoroughly clean the airbrush. With my favorite Paasche H-3 external-mix airbrush, cleaning requires only spraying thinner (water for acrylic colors) through the airbrush color control until it comes out clear, then gently swabbing the inside with a Q-Tip and a pipe cleaner. Needle-type internal-mix airbrushes require some disassembly for cleaning, and you should always pull the needle to remove all traces of paint.

Finish by cleaning all the gear that was touched by paint: color cups or siphons, strainers, eye-droppers, bottles, and so on. Cleanliness is indeed next to godliness when it comes to maintaining your airbrush and achieving good results with it, and the cleanup operation is actually the most important aspect of preparing for your next airbrushing session.

AIRBRUSHING POLLY S

Polly S acrylic colors have been around for at least 20 years, and I can't tell you how many times I've been told they can't be airbrushed. That's rubbish, and I've seen dozens of models with beautifully sprayed Polly S finishes.

The first consideration in using Polly S is cleaning the model. Unlike enamels and lacquers, water-based paints won't cut through finger oils or residues left from molding the plastic. Clean plastic models with liquid dishwashing detergent followed by rinsing with lots of clear water, then put the model aside to dry. Try not to touch it again until it's been painted and had time to cure thoroughly.

Thin the paint 50-50 with automobile windshield-washer solvent, the blue stuff that comes in gallon jugs at your service station. I've also used a half-and-half mixture of isopropyl alcohol and water as the thinner, with good results. After thinning — and this is important — strain the paint through a fine tea strainer.

Raise the output pressure from your compressor a pound or two, test your spray pattern on scrap, and spray the model. Polly S dries fast, so cleaning the spraying equipment is even more critical than with other types of paint. The thinned paint can't be returned to the Polly S bottle; either store it in a separate bottle or throw it away.

AIRBRUSHING ACCU-FLEX ACRYLIC COLORS

The Accu-Flex line of paints from Badger provides a thin, tough finish, the closest thing I've seen in a water-based paint to my old favorite, Floquil Railroad Colors. But the new paint requires a few new wrinkles for successful airbrush application. Here are three tips I've come up with:

1. Thinning. Accu-Flex recommends using the paint straight from the bottle. You can thin it slightly with water only, but even a trace of alcohol will turn it to a gooey mess. That rules out windshield-washer solvent, too. Unused thinned paint must be discarded.

2. Spraying. The paint dries so quickly that it tends to build up in the airbrush tip and clog. Stop spraying every 10 minutes or so and thoroughly rinse the airbrush with a solution of ammonia and warm water. This is the same solution to use for post-spraying cleanup, and to remove paint from the model before it has fully cured. Once the Accu-Flex paint cures overnight it's just about impossible to remove.

3. Cleanup. This paint is almost bulletproof after drying, and that means even small traces can weld your airbrush into a useless mass. Spray lots and lots of water through the color tip, then spray some more! My spray booth is right next to the laundry tub, so I actually hold the airbrush under a stream of warm water for a couple of minutes while spraying to clean it.

PICKING LINT OUT OF A WET FINISH

The paint is going on like glass when you spot a curly piece of lint plumb in the middle of your pride and joy. Make a loop of masking tape with the sticky side facing out, then gently dab at the lint until you can lift it off the surface. Then continue airbrushing and no one will ever know about the disaster that you averted.

SAVING YOUR PAINT FROM THE AIR

Our model paints are formulated to dry or cure upon contact with air. Trouble is, as soon as you use some of the paint, you leave a certain amount of air in the bottle, in contact with the paint. Sooner or later you'll come back to use the paint again and find a clinker — the paint plus the air has gone solid on you, and you need a new bottle. This always happens on Sunday night when the hobby shop is closed.

It's a problem that can't be cured entirely, but there are a couple of tactics you can try to keep good paint from going bad. The first is to pour the paint into progressively smaller bottles as you use it up. I keep a supply of clean 1/2-ounce Floquil and Polly S bottles on hand so I can transfer paint to them as I deplete the standard 1-ounce bottles.

SAVING YOUR PAINT FROM THE AIR — II

The second trick is to add some inert mass to the paint to make up for the missing volume and displace the air. I've used glass marbles, and I've read about modelers using fat sheet-metal screws, but virtually anything that won't react with the paint and will help fill up the bottle will do the job.

USING BB SHOT TO MARK YOUR PAINT

Anytime you do anything to alter the paint in a bottle or tin, add a single metal BB shot to the container. That way, you can tell the pure, unaltered colors from those you've thinned for spraying or otherwise changed. This keeps your full-strength "base" colors identified and prevents you from mixing colors that you won't be able to duplicate later.

I've also used this marking tactic to manage my considerable inventory of enamels and lacquers. With over 150 bottles of one brand on hand, using the BB to indicate thinning means I can return thinned paint to the original bottle instead of maintaining separate thinned and full-strength supplies. The BB tells me that I've modified the paint in the past, so I don't over-thin or add too much glaze. (Never return thinned water-base paints like Polly S or Accu-Flex to the bottle — it will make the whole bottle go bad.)

THE HANDIEST TOOL — WATER PUMP PLIERS

One of the handiest tools around my paint bench is a pair of long-handled water pump pliers. They're used every day to remove the tops of paint bottles. Because the jaws are adjustable they can be used on a wide variety of jars and bottles.

PRIMER FOR SILVER PAINT

Most of our railroad models can be airbrushed without first applying a primer coat, and I confess I don't often use one. My biggest exception, however, is a model that will have a silver finish. Silver paints don't cover well, especially over black styrene, and you'll need to apply either a white or light gray primer before the final metallic coating.

DECALS FOR CRISP PAINTED WINDOWS

Faced with painting two dozen identical clerestory windows on a not-quite-crisply molded passen-

ger car roof, I hit upon the idea of applying rectangular pieces of black decal material. I applied a gloss coating to the window area, cut uniform 6"-wide strips of decal, and applied them over the irregular openings, including over a couple of windows that were behind protruding smokejacks.

The uniform width of the painted-on windows actually helps the model look more uniform than it is. The result is far better than hand painting could ever do, because you can prod the rectangular pieces of decal around with a brush or tweezers. The same technique is excellent for adding labels and warning placards to barrels and crates.

INCOMPATIBILITY: TESTOR DULLCOTE AND ALCOHOL

I've found out the hard way that Testor Dullcote, the flattest flat clear finish, is incompatible with alcohol, both rubbing and denatured. Models coated with Dullcote will turn frosty white if you try to clean off a spot with alcohol, or if you use a weathering formula that includes alcohol. Don't do it!

TESTING, TESTING, TESTING!

Time marches on and on, and the longer you build models the more often you'll run up against old paint, glues, and decals around your workshop. Is it still good? Will it dry? Will those markings stick and settle down against the surface of the model?

There's no better advice than "When in doubt, test it!" Try spraying the paint to see that it dries, test the glue on some scrap model parts, and apply a section of decal on a derelict carbody. The alternative is having a model that you've lavished many hours on go bad because of old paint, glue, or markings, and that's simply not worth considering. After all, this is supposed to be fun!

This HO cannery from Builders in Scale includes parts colored using many of the techniques in this chapter. All the metal parts were airbrushed, and virtually every surface received the standard wash and dry-brush treatment.

This 10-stall roundhouse on the C&DR was kitbashed from several Revell HO enginehouse kits. It was a big project to begin with, but it would have been even bigger if it hadn't been possible to cast the doors and smokejacks using Alumilite casting compound.

10
Workshop tips

Using tools, adhesives, and materials to build detailed models

IF THE LAYOUT IS THE STAGE where the drama of model railroading takes place, then the workbench is the dressing room where actors are readied for their roles. This final chapter is devoted to techniques and materials you'll find helpful in your backstage area.

A STAND-UP WORKBENCH FOR SIT-DOWN WORKERS

Do you sit all day, then come home only to sit again to work on your hobby? I did, and my once-boyish physique was starting to show it. More than 10 years ago I built a stand-up workbench, with the top 45½" from the floor. This height allows me to work standing up, which I find comfortable most of the time. It also brings the workbench top and the work closer to my ceiling-mounted fluorescent lamp, giving me better light on the subject!

For those evenings when I'm tired I have a tall stool for working seated at my high bench. But after years of standing up, I actually feel awkward sitting!

AN OUTDOOR WORKBENCH FOR AN INDOOR HOBBY

Once summer comes along most of us throttle back on modeling, but there's always a warm, clear summer afternoon when your mind drifts toward the workbench. If the lawn's mown and the car doesn't need washing, I like to have a couple of simple projects that I can work on outdoors. Usually my outdoor modeling involves doing preliminary work on kit parts that I'll complete later, indoors.

Here's a list of typical outdoor jobs:

- ❏ Prepare castings (heavy ones won't blow away)
- ❏ Build trees
- ❏ Build vehicle kits (even in National Parks!)
- ❏ Rough-sand resin structure walls

Keep in mind that anything that involves gluing is hard, because glue dries almost too fast when you're out in the sunshine.

PAINTING YOUR WORKBENCH TOP

For years my workbench top was plywood, or more exactly, plywood colored by the various paints that I'd spilled on it. After spilling a whole bottle of flat white and noticing how easy that made it to find black styrene parts, I tried painting the entire top with flat white latex paint.

That was 10 years ago, and ever since I've rolled and brushed on a coat of flat white about twice a year. The job gives me an excuse to clean off and dust the bench every six months, and covering up all the spills and cuts seems to make new projects go better, too.

A NEWSPRINT PAD ON YOUR WORKBENCH

Especially for painting tasks, I find a big 24" x 30" newsprint sketching pad is an excellent working surface. You can sop paint out of a brush on the pad, and when it becomes soiled, you simply tear off the top sheet and start with a fresh, clean working surface.

PAPER TOWEL DISPENSERS WHERE YOU NEED THEM

One of the best moves I ever made was to mount a cheap plastic holder for a roll of paper towels on the ceiling over my workbench and another one near my basement sink, which is right next to my spray booth. Both locations are perfect for routine use — and better yet for emergencies, such as a spilled bottle of paint or glue. Just be sure to keep a fresh roll of towels in each holder: There's no worse feeling than reaching up and grabbing a bare roll core!

A WORKBENCH TRASH CAN OF YOUR OWN

Whether your workbench is a permanent setup or a kitchen table, think about setting up a special trash can for it. The can should be off limits to kids so they won't find knife blades or half bottles of paint, and it may be a good idea to keep a cover on it. If you can't establish such a waste container, keep an old mayonnaise jar on your bench for disposing of these "hazardous" modeling wastes.

WORK OVER THE TRASH CAN

My workbench trash can is 28" tall, which allows me to work on messy jobs right over it. I set up the barrel next to workbench, hold the work on top, and

go at it. Remembering this is especially handy when you're working with Styrofoam for making scenery sections or liftouts.

VACUUM WHILE YOU WORK!

Someday I'm going to have a better setup, but as I write this my workbench is located in the same room as my layout. This means that dust-producing operations like sanding wood, grinding on plaster, or slimming down resin building walls takes place right where the dust winds up on the railroad — a perfect recipe for dirty track and dusty trees!

The ultimate solution, of course, is to move, but an interim solution to keep most of the dust off the railroad is to clamp the shop vac hose in the bench vise and work with the vacuum running. Wetting the shop vac filter will keep even more dust inside the vac — and off your railroad.

PROJECT TRAYS

I keep half a dozen shallow project trays around my workshop to hold unassembled parts and organize instructions and notes. Usually they're made from the top or bottom of a good-sized kit box. These trays help prevent projects from becoming mingled — and if you don't work every project straight through from start to finish, they also provide assistance in remembering where you were last time you worked on the model.

CARDBOARD SLABS FOR CUTTING

The backing from a used-up writing pad makes a good disposable cutting surface for your workbench. I try to keep several of them around, and when one becomes too chopped up to do its job, into the trash it goes.

CARDBOARD SQUARES FOR MIXING

It's handy to keep a small pile of scrap cardstock squares on workbench. I cut up old Christmas gift boxes into 2" squares with my paper cutter, then use them for jobs like mixing epoxy or dispensing a few drops of glue. If you or a friend have changed jobs or titles, old business cards are just the ticket for this sort of use.

TRANSFERRING MEASUREMENTS

An easy way to transfer dimensions from full-size templates to the material for a model is to lay the drawings over the material, then push a sharp sewing needle through the drawings at critical points such as edges, corners, and peaks. Connect the appropriate marks with a fine-point 4-H pencil, then cut out the parts.

USING DIVIDERS TO TRANSFER MEASUREMENTS TO THE WORK

A pair of dividers is a must on your workbench for transferring all types of measurements from one surface to another. They're especially useful for marking repeated dimensions like the width of individual hand grabs or the distance between the holes for stirrup steps on freight cars.

MULTIPLE SCRAP BOXES

The oldest saw in modeling is that parts "came from my scrap box," and one of the secrets of modeling is saving scraps from everything you build. You'll save time and effort if you sort your one scrap box into several: I separate stripwood, sheetwood, wire, castings, styrene scraps, styrene sheet, and — well, you get the idea. Being able to reach for the kind of scrap you need when you need it is more than a big help — it keeps you from sorting through everything you own over and over again.

AN INVENTORY OF STYRENE STRIPS

One of the best investments I ever made was buying an extensive inventory of Evergreen styrene strips. The cost was roughly the same as for an inexpensive brass engine, and I purchased one package of every size.

If you like to build models, it's a great luxury to have all the sizes on hand. When you need a certain size, you can find it and use it instead of cursing that you don't have it. Your hobby dealer might even be persuaded to give you some kind of break for buying 50 or so packages at a time!

This is also the kind of thing where two or more guys could go together to split packages so everyone could have two or three strips of each size.

A FAST-AND-EASY FLASH REMOVER

A brass-bristled rotary brush in a battery-powered motor tool helps remove flash quickly and easily from plastic castings, especially thin flash on small parts that are hard to hold.

The brass brush is also the ideal tool for removing paint from plastic parts where they will be cemented. As long as you use the battery-powered motor tool the brush won't melt the plastic, and it won't hurt your fingers, either.

FROM THE OPERATING ROOM

Hemostats, those surgical clamps that look like scissors, are great for holding small parts while painting, gluing or soldering. They can be held in your hand or positioned in a bench vise. Several specialty tool vendors have them, including Micro-Mark.

AND FROM YOUR DENTIST!

I've got half a dozen stainless-steel dental picks with various tips in my tool stand, and they often come in handy. They're great for carving plaster, scraping away excess solder, or sculpting fine detail in epoxy putty masters. I bought mine used at a big-city hardware store, but I've seen them advertised by some of the mail-order tool companies, and you may be able to obtain a few worn-out examples from your dentist just for the asking.

TINY PIN VISES

If you do a lot of drilling with really small drills in the No. 70-80 range, the trick to getting more than a couple of holes from each drill bit is to use a lightweight, really tiny pin vise. I have a couple of them — I think they're available from Micro-Mark — that are so small and light that I can let go of them while drilling a No. 80 hole and the drill bit is strong enough to support them.

As a result of this trick, I have some No. 78, 79, and 80 drills that have a couple of years of occasional use to their credit. Considering that these drill bits cost at least a buck apiece these days, the little pin vises are a bargain!

USE FILES THAT ARE BIG ENOUGH!

One of the biggest mistakes you can make is to use files that are too small for the job. A lot of modelers think they have everything they need when they purchase a set of 12 needle files, but needle files, being quite fine, take roughly forever if there's more than a trace of material to be removed.

When you're trying to true up straight edges you need a larger file, otherwise you get a lot of little peaks and valleys along the edge. It's important that the file itself be longer than the edge being filed.

For cleaning up castings I use an 8" single-cut flat mill file. This removes material quickly, doesn't clog, and goes a long way toward making those straight edges needed on even medium-size parts.

A HAIR DRYER TO SPEED THINGS UP

You can make paint, glue, or decals dry faster by using a hair dryer set on medium heat. I don't recommend it for every project, but that blast of warm air can come in handy for last-minute work the night before a contest or a layout visit. Careful now, don't melt anything!

TAPE OVER THAT "WRONG" END

I don't even like to think of how many times I've tried to tighten the collet of a Dremel motor-tool with the wrong end of the double-ended wrench furnished with the tool. If you don't try any other tip in this book, try this one: Cut a strip of duct tape and wrap it around the wrong end. The tape'll take about 20 years to wear out (after all, you never use that end), and you'll never try to use the wrench backwards again.

A TOOL THAT WORKS BETTER WITHOUT THE HANDLE

If you've been building wood kits for a while you know that distressing the wood with a brass-bristled suede brush is a great way to add character. Nowadays most suede brushes come with handles that extend away from the bristles, and I find that the brush is easier to control without the handle. Saw it off and file the edges smooth, and you'll find that the brush works better for distressing wood or removing fuzz from razor saw cuts on plastic walls.

A BENT-NEEDLE APPLICATOR FOR SUPER GLUE

One of my favorite homemade tools has always been a robust sewing needle (darning needles are best) mounted in a length of 1/4" birch dowel. Like No. 11 hobby knives, I keep half a dozen of them on my workbench so I can't possibly lose them all.

These probes are handy for applying just a single

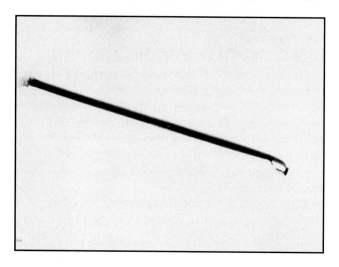

drop of white or yellow glue exactly where I want it, but when it comes to applying super glues the needle is too fine to hold enough glue. Grinding or breaking off the tip of the needle eye provides a fixture to capture single drops of glue, but my favorite modification is to bend the tip of the needle almost 90 degrees. This gives you a hook that will hold just enough glue for controlled application.

SOPPING AWAY EXCESS SUPER GLUE

I love super glue, and in the 20-plus years I've been using it the only problem is how to apply just enough, especially of the water-thin "original formula" stuff that I use most often.

What I usually wind up doing is applying just a little extra glue, then immediately sopping away the excess with rolled-up paper towel "twirls." Make these by tearing off a small piece of paper towel and twisting it into a tight cone. The twirl is perfect for soaking up the extra glue quickly, after which you toss it out and make another one.

SUPER-GLUE REMOVERS

If you're going to use super glue (ACC), you need at least one kind of debonder available on your workbench — preferably where you can reach it with one hand stuck to a model or the bench top. I suggest

keeping two kinds on hand: a small bottle of acetone — which dissolves the glue quickly but will also dissolve styrene and other plastics — and a dispenser of the debonder formula offered for your favorite brand, most of which are water-soluble and won't ruin plastic parts.

DIFFERENT PLASTIC CEMENTS FOR DIFFERENT JOBS

It helps to have at least two kinds of solvent-type plastic cement on your workbench: fast and slow. I use a fast-drying liquid plastic cement such as Micro-Weld, Tenax 7R, or IPS Weld-On #4 for most styrene assembly, but substitute the slower Testor's Liquid Cement for joints where more strength or more time to adjust and align the parts is required.

CUSTOM-BLENDED PLASTIC CEMENTS

Once your arsenal of glues includes fast- and slow-setting solvent-type plastic cements, you can blend them to come up with in-between setting times. Try combining equal parts of a fast-setting cement like MicroScale Micro-Weld or Tenax 7-R with Testor's Liquid Plastic Cement and see if you like the results. Be sure to keep track of the proportions so you can duplicate your favorite formula.

BUYING MEK BY THE GALLON

A tiny bottle of fast-setting liquid plastic cement at the hobby shop will set you back three or four bucks, but a whole gallon of methyl-ethyl-ketone (MEK) at the hardware store is about $15. It's great for most styrene cementing jobs, and it's a good solvent for routine cleanup jobs, too. Buying a gallon becomes even more reasonable if you split the gallon (or quart) with a modeling buddy.

QUICK-GRAB ADHESIVE

Different hobbies seem to have their own tools and materials, and there's usually little crossover. The dollhouse folks have been using a tube-type

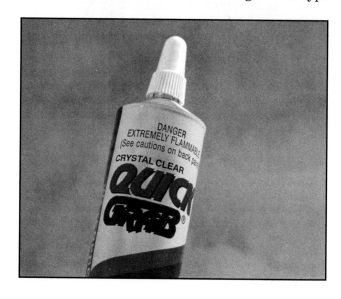

cement called Quick Grab for years. It's a clear, thick, solvent-based adhesive that's used as a contact cement. Spread a little on both surfaces and push together, pull apart, allow to dry 30 or 40 seconds, then push together for good. It will stick almost anything to anything, and I use it where dissimilar materials need to be joined. It's great for installing window glazing in structures.

Excess Quick Grab can be removed with nail polish remover or acetone. You'll find it in craft and hobby shops in 1.5-oz. tubes.

STYROFOAM-COMPATIBLE ADHESIVES

Several adhesives are suitable for Styrofoam:

Epoxy resins, including the Everfix brand, won't hurt Styrofoam scenery.

White and yellow wood glues in various colors and brands dry slowly, but they're all about the same as far as Styrofoam is concerned.

Elmer's water-soluble contact cement works great! Just brush it on each piece to be joined, wait 5 or 10 minutes (until it changes color), and push the pieces together. Only dynamite will get them apart.

Liquid Nails construction adhesive is the least expensive glue that is Styrofoam-compatible. There are dozens of construction adhesives on the market, so make sure you read the label. It must say it's safe for Styrofoam.

SURFACING FILLER PUTTY WITH SUPER GLUE

Automotive filler putty is handy stuff even in this

high-tech world, and a tube of 3M Red or Blue or some Squadron Green putty still ranks a spot in my bag of tricks. While they shape and sand quickly, these putties are meant to be used with heavy sandable auto primers, which fill in their porous surface in preparation for additional primer and color coats.

If you don't want the bother of multiple primer coats, try this. Apply filler putty as normal, let dry, and file and sand to shape. (These putties work especially well with wet-or-dry sandpaper used wet; if you haven't tried wet sanding, you'll be amazed at how quickly wet sanding smooths a rough surface.)

Rinse the sanding dust from the surface with plenty of water, sand more if necessary, then wipe the surface dry and let it air dry for at least half an hour. Then apply a light coating of thin super glue, allowing it to sink into the putty. Wet sand again with fine-grit paper — and do it right away; the longer super glue cures, the harder it gets.

The super glue will seal the surface for painting, as well as adding a hard finish that's virtually identical to styrene.

HOMEMADE PLASTIC FILLER

Dissolve shards of scrap plastic sprue in lacquer thinner or MEK to make your own filler paste or texture putty. Figure modelers often brush on this "liquid plastic" to build up clothing contours slowly. Although it takes a long time to dry (overnight, usually more), this filler is easy to texture with a blade, dental pick, or hot knife.

ALUMILITE AND RTV FOR CASTING MULTIPLE PARTS

Casting your own detail parts is a bit beyond the scope of this book, but a few comments here could be sufficient to get you started. About 5 years ago Alumilite, an easy-to-use buff-colored casting resin, appeared on the scene. It's one of a broad family of plastic resins, but what makes it uniquely useful is that it's widely available for hobby use, and it sets fast.

If you have special parts that you need multiple duplicates of (for example, the doors and smokejacks on the enginehouse on page 87), it's worth carefully making a master pattern, then making an RTV (Room Temperature Vulcanizing) rubber mold of it. (Castolite is a good source for small quantities of RTV rubber; see Addresses.)

The Alumilite comes with excellent directions and tips, but here are a few more. First, painting the surfaces of the RTV molds with full-strength Floquil Railroad Colors will accomplish three purposes: (1) the paint will serve as a mold-release agent, (2) the paint coating will help the mold last longer, and (3) the Alumilite will bond to the paint, pre-coloring the parts you make.

Second, you can make excellent parts with Alumilite using the "squash" process, where the fluid resin is poured into one mold half and the second mold half is simply pushed into the first. An even better way is to "butter" each mold half with resin, then firmly push them together and hold until

the resin cures in just a few minutes.

The third tip is the handiest of all. Chilling the two parts of the Alumilite resin in a refrigerator gives you significantly longer pot life — or working time — than using the material at room temperature. I keep my Alumilite in a small refrigerator beneath my workbench, where it's always ready to make a needed part.

A DOZEN TIPS ON WORKBENCH CHEMICALS

Model railroading is not supposed to be better living through chemistry, but here's an assortment of common solvents and chemicals and what they are good for around your shop. Most them can be found in hardware stores and home centers in sizes from a pint to a gallon, and they're usually bargains compared to what we pay for small quantities bottled for hobby use:

Acetone is a strong solvent cleaner for metal that can substitute in a pinch for solvent-type plastic cement. It works well as a debonder for super glue.

Brake fluid will loosen and remove several types of paint, usually without damaging the underlying metal or plastic surface. Always test brake fluid on an unseen surface of the model before dipping the whole thing into it.

Carbo-Chlor is a nonflammable solvent and spot remover, a modern substitute for carbon tetrachloride (which turned out to be poisonous). It's a good degreaser and cleaner for metal parts and electrical items.

Denatured (methyl) alcohol is my favorite before-painting washing treatment for plastic and metal models and parts. It also removes certain types of paint; the paint on old Bachmann models seems to react to it (and nothing else). If you spill your bottle of decal-setting solvent the night before the big contest, you can dilute denatured alcohol with a water and make an acceptable substitute.

Dio-Sol is Floquil's proprietary thinner for its Railroad Colors line. It contains xylene, a hydrocarbon solvent that is dangerous enough to require respirators and heavy-duty exhaust fans, and it smells like lacquer thinner, but don't try to substitute lacquer thinner for it. Dio-Sol contains other compounds in addition to solvents, and using solvents alone can cause the paints to go bad. I use only Dio-Sol for thinning, and lacquer thinner for cleaning brushes and airbrushes.

Isopropyl alcohol is a good solvent for weathering treatments. Mixed with India ink it makes a good shadow wash and detail darkener. You'll find it in two strengths at your pharmacy, 70 percent and 91 percent, and to tell the truth I can't tell the difference between them for hobby use.

Lacquer thinner is a good cleanup solvent for enamel and lacquer paints, but don't use it to thin Floquil Railroad Colors. It also works as a slow solvent cement for styrene.

Methyl-ethyl-ketone (MEK) is a strong solvent and makes a good fast-setting cement for styrene and other plastics. It's also a good paint stripper and degreaser for metal parts.

Mineral spirits is the modern-day (and less smelly) substitute for turpentine. It's the preferred thinner for enamel paints like Testor Model Master colors, and it's also the stuff to use to prepare washes with flat enamels or artist's oil paints.

Muriatic acid is dilute (but still pretty strong) hydrochloric acid. You can use it to clean brass for painting or before soldering, and in a pinch it can be used as soldering flux for non-electrical jobs. Usually it's used for cleaning stains off concrete, so you need to be careful with it: Rubber gloves and safety glasses are mandatory. After treating metal with it, scrub with water-and-detergent solution and rinse with lots of water.

Oven cleaner (a common brand is Easy-Off) is sodium hydroxide, or caustic soda (lye). This is rubber-gloves-and-safety-glasses stuff, too, but it does a super job stripping old paint off models, especially metal ones.

Windshield washer solvent, the blue stuff available at your service station for under $2 a gallon, is a good cleaning agent for preparing models for Polly S and other water-based acrylic paints, and can be used as an airbrush thinner for several of them. Once mixed with paint, either use the paint or throw it out. The solvent consists of water, alcohol as a wetting agent, and detergent.

Where to find the products

Alumilite casting compound
Alumilite Corp.
 P.O. Box 310
 Richland, MI 49083-1259
Boat kits (HO)
J.D. Innovations
 P.O. Box 110448
 Aurora, CO 80042
Castolite (RTV molding rubbers)
 4915 Dean Street
 Woodstock, IL 60098
Celluclay Paper Mache
Activa Products
 P.O. Box 472
 Westford, MA 01886
Decal-setting solutions
MicroScale Industries, Inc.
 P.O. Box 11950
 Costa Mesa, CA 92627
Dullcote clear flat finish
The Testor Corporation
 620 Buckbee St.
 Rockford, IL 61104
Durham's Water Putty
Donald Durham Co.
 P.O. Box 804
 Des Moines, IA 50304
Envirotex decoupage resin
(for modeling water)
Environmental Technologies, Inc.
 P.O. Box 365
 Fields Landing, CA 95537
Fence kit (HO)
Central Valley
 1203 Pike Lane
 Oceano, CA 93445
Flexwax
American Art Clay Co.
 4717 W. 16th. St.
 Indianapolis, IN 46222
Ground foam scenic textures
AMSI Scale Model Supplies
 115-B Bellam Boulevard
 P.O. Box 3497
 San Rafael, CA 94912
Timber Products
 2029 E. Howe Ave.
 Tempe AZ 85281
Woodland Scenics
 P.O. Box 98
 Linn Creek, MO 65052
Gypsolite first-coat plaster
(This is a product of Gold Bond and

sold at builder's and masonry supply companies. A very similar product, Structolite, is made by U.S. Gypsum and distributed nationwide.)
Heki-dur building material
U.S. Exclusive importer:
Portman Hobby Distributors
 851 Washington St.
 Peekskill, NY 10566
Hydrocal
Tooling and Casting Division
United States Gypsum Co.
 101 S. Wacker Dr.
 Chicago, IL 60606
**Instant Buildings
background flats**
Wm. K. Walthers Inc.
 5601 W. Florist Ave.
 Milwaukee, WI 53218
Junkyard detail piles
Chooch Enterprises, Inc.
 8547 152nd Ave. N.E.
 Redmond, WA 98052
Komatex plastic
Kommerling USA Inc.
 210 Summit Ave.
 Montvale, NJ 07645
Lobster traps (photoetched)
Builders in Scale
 P.O. Box 441432-A
 Aurora, CO 80044
Micro Krystal-Klear
(see decal setting solutions, above)
Mini-Hold dollhouse wax
Handcraft Designs, Inc.
 Hatfield, PA 19440
MV Products lenses
 P.O. Box 6622
 Orange, CA 92613
Northeastern eye pins
 P.O. Box 727
 Methuen, MA 01844
**Patina-It copper
weathering solution**
A-West
 4050 Leicester Dr.
 Kennesaw, GA 30144
Pine trees
High Pines, Ltd.
 2015 Garst Circle
 Boone, IA 50036
**Perma-Scene
scenery compound**

Permacraft Products, Inc.
 P.O. Box 81142
 Cleveland, OH 44181
Punched-paper leaves
K & S Scenery Products
 P.O. Box 117824
 Carrollton, TX 75011-7824
Quick Grab adhesive
Quick Grab, Inc.
 P.O. Box 490
 Manlius, NY 13104
Rustall weathering system
Kuras Design Group
 112 Point Lobos Ave.
 San Francisco, CA 94121
**Rigid Wrap plaster-
impregnated gauze**
Activa Products (address above)
Rock molds
Woodland Scenics (address above)
Scenery supplies, general
Express Model
Landscaping Supplies
 P.O. Box 1594
 Greensburg, PA 15601-6594
Sculpey Modeling Compound
Polyform Products
 9420 Byron St.
 Schiller Park, IL 60176
Sculptamold
American Art Clay Co.
 4717 W. 16th St.
 Indianapolis, IN 46222
Shingles
Precision Lasercraft
 32 Beekman Drive
 Agawam, MA 01001
Campbell Scale Models
 P.O. Box 5307
 Durango, CO 81301
Signs (photocopied color)
Classic Signs Ltd.
 P.O. Box 1073
 San Carlos, CA 94070-9998
SS Ltd. detail parts
JAKS Industries
 P.O. Box 1421S
 Golden, CO 80402
**Styrene strip, sheet,
and sidewalk material**
Evergreen Scale Models
 12808 N.E. 125th Way
 Kirkland, WA 98034

Always check first at your local hobby shop before writing or calling direct to the manufacturer.

Bibliography

When it comes to good information on model railroad scenery and structures, this book doesn't even begin to scratch the surface. These are suggestions on where to look for more good ideas than we had room to present here:

CHAPTER 1. SCENERY TIPS

How to Build Realistic Model Railroad Scenery, 2nd Edition, by Dave Frary. Published in 1991 by Kalmbach Publishing Co. (see inside back cover of this book). This 12-chapter cookbook of model railroad scenery techniques is the bible of the water-soluble scenery techniques most modelers use today.

CHAPTER 2. TIPS FOR TEXTURE AND TREES

Scenery Tips and Techniques from Model Railroader. Published in 1989 by Kalmbach, this compilation of articles from *Model Railroader* includes numerous short features on texture materials and techniques for modeling trees.

CHAPTER 3. FORCED PERSPECTIVE AND BACKDROPS

Scenery Tips, (above), includes several features on this topic.

CHAPTER 4. ON THE WATERFRONT

Boat Modeling the Easy Way, a Scratch Builder's Guide, by Harold H. "Dynamite" Payson. Published in 1993 by International Marine, P.O. Box 220, Camden, ME 04843. This book on building large-scale boats and ships from wood includes plans for 10 vintage watercraft.

CHAPTER 5. TRICKS WITH FIGURES AND VEHICLES

Building and Painting Scale Figures, by Sheperd Paine, published by Kalmbach in 1993, is a detailed treatise on figure modeling by a master of the craft. Focused mainly on larger-scale military figure modeling, the book includes a chapter on techniques applicable to small-scale figures.

The Narrow Gauge and Short Line Gazette, published six times a year, runs articles on vintage vehicle modeling. The *Gazette* is available from hobby shops, or direct from the publisher, Benchmark Publications, Ltd., P.O. Box 26, Los Altos, CA 94023.

CHAPTER 6. DETAILING AND SUPERDETAILING

Detailing Tips and Techniques from Model Railroader. Published in 1993 by Kalmbach, this compilation of articles from *Model Railroader* focuses on modeling detailed scenes, especially highly detailed urban settings.

Up Clear Creek on the Narrow Gauge, by Harry W. Brunk, published in 1990 by Benchmark Publications (address above). This compilation of 54 articles from the *Gazette* tells how the author modeled the Colorado & Southern narrow gauge in HOn3. The book includes techniques on virtually all aspects of layout building, plus substantial doses of Harry Brunk's sensible homespun modeling philosophy.

CHAPTER 7. SIGNS OF LIFE

The Fabulous Franklin & South Manchester Railroad, by George Sellios, published in 1991 by Fine Scale Miniatures, 49 Main St., Peabody, MA 01906. The master of HO city modeling shows all and tells a lot about his techniques and philosophy in this self-published, all-color pictorial, with photos by Dave Frary. George's techniques with signs are easily worth the price of the book.

CHAPTER 8. IMPROVING AND DETAILING STRUCTURES

222 Tips for Building Model Railroad Structures, by Dave Frary, published in 1992 by Kalmbach. In a format identical to this book, Dave rolls out tips and techniques for improving wood, plastic, metal, and plaster structure kits, plus a hefty helping of down-to-earth workshop wisdom.

CHAPTER 9. WEATHERING AND AIRBRUSHING

Painting and Finishing Scale Models, by Paul Boyer, published in 1991 by Kalmbach. Although aimed at plastic and military modelers, this compilation of articles from *FineScale Modeler* magazine is the best available how-to-do-it presentation on the basics of airbrushing. Also includes a comprehensive discussion of decal application and related finishing techniques.

CHAPTER 10. WORKSHOP TIPS

See *222 Tips for Building Model Railroad Structures* (above).

How-to-do-it videotapes on scenery building featuring author Dave Frary are available from The Trackside Modeler, P.O. Box 333, Swampscott, MA 01907-3333. These tapes include hands-on demonstrations of the techniques used to create many of the scenes shown in this book. Write for current pricing information.

Index

A

Accenting with texture, 51
Accu-Flex paint, airbrushing, 84
Acetone, 10, 92
Acrylics, for dry-brushing, 80
Addresses, 93
Airbrushes:
   Air pressures, 82
   Bottles, 83
   Holder, 83
   Choosing, 81
Airbrushing routine, 83
Airbrushing, 81-84
Alumilite, 87, 91, 93
Americanizing trucks, 45
Apple Barrel paints, 81
Asphalt shingles, 71

B

Backdating structures, 72
Backdrops:
   Cracks, fixing, 30
   Flats, 28
   Height, 29
   Painting, 29
   Temporary, 31
   Two-layer, 29
Backwards buildings, 72
Barbed wire, 51
Barrels, 48
Bending buildings, 74
Bibliography, 94
Birch trees, 24
Black and white signs, 61
Blacktop road, 8
Black wash formulas, 12
Boat and ships:
   Hulls, 35
   HO scale, source for, 37
   Listing to port or starboard, 36
Boulders, 9
Boulders, Sculptamold, 8
Brake fluid, 92
Brick, coloring with chalk, 67
Bridge abutments, 15
Bridges, weathering, 79
Building board, 64
Bumpy chenille trees, 23

C

Canvas tarps, 44
Carbo-Chlor, 92
Cardboard mockups, 64
Cardboard slabs and squares, 88
Cars, track cleaning, 54, 55
Carving Durham's Water Putty, 14
Cast-metal buildings, painting, 73
Casting detail parts, 91
Castings, buffing, 67
Castings, installing temporarily, 67
Ceiling color, 29
Cement-block walls, 15
Cheap detail, 50
Chemical carving, 9

Chemicals, workbench, 92
Chimneys, soot streaks, 69
Choosing colors, 11
Chrome trim, 45
Cleaning old structure, 76
Cleaning track, 53
Clouds, 31
Color-copier signs, 61
Color-scheme buildings, 64
Colors, choosing, 11
Colors, for scenic foam, 16
Compressor for airbrushing, 82
Concrete platforms, 67
Copper roof flashing, 70
Crowd modeling, 42
Crude detail, 48

D

Daisy fields, 18
Dave's Fish & Chips, 76
Dead trees, 20
Decals:
   Sign kit, 61
   For windows, 85
   How to apply, 59
   Making signs with, 58
   On inside of windows, 61
   That explode, 61
   That won't stick, 60
Deformed buildings, 72
Delicate details, 50
Denatured alcohol, 92
Dental picks, 89
Detailing, 47
Diamond-pattern shingles, 71
Diesel crud, 78
Dio-Sol, 92
Dirt, for texture, 17
Dividers for transferring measurement, 88
Doors, replacing, 75
Downtown buildings, 65
Drips, modeling, 35
Dry-brushing, 80
Dry transfers, 57, 59
Dulling Polly S paints, 12
Durham's Water Putty, carving, 14
Dust on waterfront, removing, 36

E

Easternizing structure, 76
Elephants, 5
Envirotex, for water, 33
Era, signs to establish, 57

F

Fences, 52
   Barbed wire, 51
Fender skirts, 46
Fiber bushes, 20
Figures, 38-42
   In vehicles, 42
Files, using right size, 89
Fishing boat conversions, 36
Fitting structures between tracks, 64
Flash remover, 89
Flexwax, 13
Flocking, 18
Floors, white glue for, 66

Flowers, 47
Foam scenery, 9
Forced perspective, 27,28
Foundations, structure, 68, 69
Free-standing details, 49

G

Gloves for spray painting, 82
Glow-in-dark signs, 62
Gluing walls, 66
Graph paper, 65
Grease strains, 78
Gypsolite scenery plaster, 7

H

Hair dryer, 89
Handles, toothpick, for painting, 67
Headlights, for vehicles, 43
Homemade plastic filler, 91
Hot-top roads, 14
Hulls, boat and ship, 35
Hydrocal scenery plaster, 7

I

Incompatibility
   Dullcote and alcohol, 85
   Pliobond and styrene, 74
Inspector general figure, 42
Introduction, 3
Isopropyl alcohol, 92

J

John Allen's track-cleaning cars, 54
Junkyard junk, 53

K

Komatex, for backdrops, 30

L

Lacquer thinner, 92
Lading piles, 49
Laser-printed signs, 61
Leaves, 19, 23
License plates, 46
Lichen sticks, 25
Lichen, substitute for, 20
Liftouts, 11
Lighting, 29
Lint, removing from wet paint, 84
Loads, for trucks, 44
Lobster traps, source, 36
Loofah sponge pine trees, 24

M

Magic wands for cleaning track, 53
Making vehicles look natural, 43
Marking thinned paint, 85
Mass-painting details, 48
Masts and spars for ships, 35
Measurements, transferring, 88
Membrane roofing, 70
Methyl-ethyl-ketone (MEK), 90, 92
Mineral spirits, 92
Model holders for painting, 83
Modifying figures, 42
Mortician's wax, 38
Motor tool wrench, 89
Mountains in Minutes foam, 9
Muriatic acid, 92

N

Nautical details, sources of, 36
Neon paint, 62

Newsprint pad, at workbench, 88

O

Oil drums, 48
Omitting details, 74
Oven cleaner, 92

P

Paint removers and thinners, 92
Painting:
    Cast-metal buildings, 73
    Figures, 39-41
    Handles, toothpick, 67
    Rail, 53
    Sand or ballast, 18
    Track, 53
Parting lines, 80
Pavement cracks, 13
Pegs for detail parts, 49
Phone poles, 52
Photo print signs, 62
Pilings, on waterfront, 34
Pin vises, 89
Pine trees, toothpick, 25
Pinning structures, 68
Pirating details, 52
Planting trees, 22
Plaster setting times, 8
Plasters, types for scenery, 7
Plastic backdrop material, 30
Plastic cements, 90
Plastic filler, homemade, 91
Platforms, concrete, 67
Pliobond incompatible with styrene, 74
Polly S, airbrushing, 84
Polly S, dulling, 12
Polyfoam, 9
Posing figures, 42
Primer, for silver paint, 85
Printed backdrops, 28
Prop, for tippy building, 75

R

Rail painting, 53
Rail size, 53
Reference photos, 32
Removable trees, 26
Respirator for spray painting, 82
Retaining walls, 15
Reviving old structure, 76
Rigging ships, 35
Roads:
    Blacktop or hot-top, 8, 14
    Pavement cracks, 13
Rocks, rubber, 13
Roofs, 69-71, 72
    Character, 70
    Cracks, filling, 70
    Detailing, 72
    Gluing, 69
    Overhang, 34
    Shingle, 69, 71
    Tin, 76
Routine for airbrushing, 83
RTV rubber molds, 91
Rust color, mixing, 80
Rustall weathering treatment, 80, 93

S

Sand, for touch-up, 18
Saving paint, 85
Saving ready-made trees, 21
Sawdust, for texture, 17
Scale effect for colors, 43, 80
Scenery, 6:
    Base materials, 7
    Plasters, 7
Scrap boxes, 89
Sculpey, 20
Sculptamold, 8:
    Boulders, 8
    Coloring, 8
    Mix for scenery, 8
    Stronger, 8
Sealing plaster castings, 67
Seaweed, coloring, 34
Setting times, plaster, changing, 8
Shiny cars, killing shine, 43
Sidewalks, 67
Signs, 56:
    Kit, decal, 61
    On buildings, 58
Silver paint, primer for, 85
Simple detailing, 50
Siphon strainers for airbrush, 83
Sky color, 12, 29
Slider cars, 54
Smoke bush trees, 23
Snags, 21
Soot streaks, 69
Spills, modeling, 35, 49, 78
Sprayers for scenery, 13
Stains and spills, 35, 49, 78
Static Grass, 18
Station platforms, 75
Station signs, 57
Stencils for making signs, 58
Sticky castings, 66
Storytelling, 3
Straining paint, 83
Straw, for texture, 17
String weeds, 19
Stripwood, thinning, 65
Structures, 63
    In trees, 26
    Leveling, 68
    Mockups, 64
Styrofoam, 7
Stumps, 20
Styrene strip inventory, 89
Styrofoam liftouts, 11
Styrofoam-compatible adhesives, 91
Suede brush, 89
Super glue, 90
    Applicator, 90
    Removers, 90
    Removing excess, 90
Surfacing filler putty, 91
Surgical clamps, 89

T

Tall grass, 19
Tape, reducing stickiness, 66

Tar, for filling roof cracks, 70
Tarpaper roofing, 70
Tarps, canvas, 44
Templates, transferring 65
Testing paints and glues, 86
Thinning oversize parts, 66
Thinning stripwood, 65
Tide line, marking and painting, 33
Tin roofs, 76
Tippy building, prop for, 75
Tires, flattening, 44
Toothpick pine trees, 25
Track:
    Cleaning, 53, 54
    Oiling, 55
    Painting, 53
Trash can for workshop, 88
Trash, in barrels, 48
Trays for projects, 88
Trees:
    Birch, 24
    Bumpy chenille, 23, 24
    Kits, 22
    Loofah sponge, 24
    Planting, 22
    Removable, 26
    Smoke bush, 23
    Woodland Scenics, 22
Trestle building, 63
Truck loads, 44
Trucks, Americanizing, 45
Tunnel portals, 14
Turntable for spray booth, 83
Two-tone paint jobs, for autos, 45

U

Upside-down bridge building, 63

V

Vacuum attachments for cleaning, 37
Vacuum for dusty jobs, 88
Vehicles, solid, 45

W

Warped walls, fixing, 66
Water: cleaning, 36
Water, modeling, 33
Water-pump pliers, 85
Watercolors for weathering, 81
Waterfront detailing, 32, 34
Weathering, 4, 78
Weathervanes, 50
Wet water, 13
Wheels, fitting, 45
Where to find the products, 93
Windshield detail, 46
Windshield-washer solvent, 92
Workbench:
    Chemicals, 92
    Outdoor, 87
    Stand-up, 87
    Top, painting, 88
Workshop tips, 87

Z

Zones, for detailing, 4